Coaching with Personal

Coaching with Personality Type

What Works

Jenny Rogers

Open University Press

Open University Press
McGraw-Hill Education
8th Floor, 338 Euston Road
London
England
NW1 3BH

email: enquiries@openup.co.uk
world wide web: www.openup.co.uk

and Two Penn Plaza, New York, NY 10121-2289, USA

First published 2017

A catalogue record of this book is available from the British Library

ISBN-13: 978-0-33-526164-2
ISBN-10: 0-33-526164-7
eISBN: 978-0-33-526165-9

Library of Congress Cataloging-in-Publication Data
CIP data applied for

Typeset by Transforma Pvt. Ltd., Chennai, India

Printed and bound by CPI Group (UK) Ltd, Croydon, CR0 4YY

Any life, no matter how long and complicated it may be, actually consists of a single moment, the moment when a person finds out once and for all who they are.

Jorge Luis Borges (1899–1986)

Dedication

For Kim, Wendi, Leni and Joe, perfect proof of the value of 'gifts differing'

Praise page

"*How can anyone resist? Coaching with Personality Type is a well written, accessible and stimulating book from one of my favourite coaching authors. Jenny brings her vast experience and warm personal style to offer the reader an in depth review of type based personality instruments from MBTI to Lumina, and how executive coaches can use type based approaches with sophistication to offer fresh insights and understanding to their clients*".

Professor Jonathan Passmore, School of Psychology,
University of Evora & Centre for Coaching,
Henley Business School, UK

"*This is the biggest book in coaching for years. The MBTI is the most widely (and wisely, and badly) used instrument in coaching, but here at last is the indispensable guide to its full proper, use in coaching and leadership development. Covers every conceivable topic, for individuals and teams, from the history to the science, the depth, wisdom, and the good pragmatic sense for which Jenny is renowned. Indispensable: thorough, comprehensive, and throughout with Jenny's trademark dry wit and pragmatism.*"

Anne Scoular, Co-Founder and Faculty Member,
Meyler Campbell, UK

"*This is the book I've been waiting for! As always, Jenny writes with great flair and humour, so reading her take on Coaching with Personality Type was a pleasure as well as immediately useful.*

I've been using the MBTI with clients for nearly 10 years now with reasonable success as a coach and coach trainer. Jenny Rogers' profound understanding of the subject and the insights she brings from her own coaching practice are illuminating, practical and inspiring. I'm really looking forward to taking this into my own coaching work and will certainly be recommending to all the coaches I work with."

Jane Cook, Head of Coaching and Leadership,
Linden Learning Ltd, UK

"A masterclass in the area. Jenny Rogers is an expert in both coaching and assessment but she avoids unnecessary statistics and theories. Rather, her book uses Jenny's in-depth knowledge to underpin rich case studies, stories and really practical insights. The majority of coaches use the type model and type measures: this book enables them to become experts in their use – and doesn't shy away from offering alternative approaches. There are plenty of type introductions around. This is the best for practising coaches by a long way."

Ian Florance, Consultant Editor, Meyler Campbell and Secretary European Test Publishers Group, UK

"As an extraordinarily well-written guide to assist both beginners and veteran coaches in the use and interpretation of the MBTI, Rogers' book has much to recommend it, and I do so wholeheartedly. It does what it says on the tin, but my goodness, it does a great deal more than that.

The section on the origins and psychological underpinnings of Type, the conceptual framework of the MBTI and its psychometric properties are presented with exemplary clarity; thorough, comprehensive and scrupulously balanced. Rogers' combination of broad brush and fine strokes makes engagement with this relatively complex subject a richly rewarding experience.

The sections on coaching, quite aside from the MBTI focus, represent a masterclass of the highest order. The author's breadth and depth of experience across a broad spectrum of individuals, organisations, and contexts, and the holistic insights thus gained, shine through on every page. Coaching with Personality Type deserves to be the gold standard, not only in respect of the MBTI and psychometric-assisted coaching, but also as an invaluable addition to the canon of coaching practice."

Neville Osrin, Emeritus Fellow, University of Exeter Business School, UK

"As a religious professional, I have used MBTI typology for many years as a tool to coach and encourage others. I believe Jenny's book to be essential reading for anyone interested in using any psychometrics in their coaching – or in their work generally. Reading it helped me correct a number of mistakes I had made. It also introduced me to many new tools to balance my practice. Her insights relating to coaching teams and the use of psychometrics will help anyone increase the effectiveness of their work with groups."

Rev. Dr. Rodney (Rod) Woods, Senior Minister, City Temple London, UK

"This book is brilliant both for those new to MBTI and for those who have been using it for years. Written in her straightforward style laced with her dry humour, Jenny informs, encourages and cautions about the possibilities of working with Type, including short case studies to demonstrate her points. She tackles head on the criticisms of the Indicator and gives an even handed write up about its competitors.

"Not just a look at the MBTI itself, Jenny provides a clear understanding of what, when, how and why a Coach might offer it as a source of data in raising the clients awareness of how they are in the world and how that may impact and influence the people around them. Great stuff!"

Liz Macann, Director, Macann
Coaching Consultancy, UK

Contents

About the author

Jenny was a pioneer of executive coaching in the UK. Her clients include senior people from a wide range of public and private sector organizations. Her book *Coaching Skills: The Definitive Guide to Being a Coach* is now in its fourth edition, has become a best-seller, is regarded as the essential book for coach training internationally and has been translated into several languages. Her books on Jungian Type Indicators and on the FIRO-B sell well internationally, and she is Series Editor of the *Coaching in Practice* series from the Open University Press/McGraw-Hill. She has a particular interest in career coaching and has published two popular books here: *Job Interview Success* and *Great Answers to Tough CV Problems*, both in 2011. *Manager as Coach: the New Way to Get Results*, co-written with Andrew Gilbert and Karen Whittleworth, was shortlisted for the Chartered Management Institute Book of the Year in 2014. *Facing Redundancy: Surviving and Thriving* gives advice on dealing with the aftermath of redundancy. *Coaching for Health*, co-written with Dr Art Maini, is a guide for healthcare professionals on using a coaching approach with patients.

As well as running her own coaching practice, Jenny supervises, teaches and trains coaches internationally. She is a full member of APECS, the UK accrediting body for senior coaches.

Acknowledgements

I am indebted to Dr Eversley Felix who first persuaded me to take an interest in the MBTI and persisted, despite my scepticism. Then to my trainers on the OPP qualifying course in the MBTI, Julie Bullen and the late Dr Susan Brock whose enthusiasm and boundless knowledge was an inspiration to me then and ever since. I thank George Davies of what was then Cambridge Management Centres, which has since become ASK Europe, for his encouragement in making what were then just draft profiles available to a wider audience in my two books of Jungian Type profiles. Helen Terry and Robert Terry of ASK have remained enthusiastic publishers of this material along with Phil Hayes and Tim Cox of my former company, Management Futures. My late husband, Alan Rogers, always believed in these books and gave me every possible encouragement, with humour and affection, to take the project to fruition.

I also thank Luke Rogers, for his patient help with graphics for this book and, as ever, for innumerable other kindnesses.

Introduction

One of the most frequent questions I am asked by newly trained coaches is, 'What other qualifications do I need to get?' Soon the next question is, 'How about the Myers–Briggs?'

This book is for coaches who want to know how and why they could incorporate personality Type questionnaires such as the Myers–Briggs Type Indicator (MBTI)®[1] or alternative Jungian instruments into their coaching. It answers questions such as, *How do I get best value out of the instrument? How do I avoid looking as if I am forcing it onto a client? How do I blend it with other instruments and approaches? How do I knit it properly into the rest of the coaching? What if the client resists?*

The first ten chapters of this book are about using these questionnaires with individuals in one-on-one coaching. The last three are about how you could make use of Type instruments in team coaching or where you are working with groups, for instance on management development courses.

In dealing with all the many questions that coaches have about using personality Type questionnaires, I do not assume that you have been fully trained in their use, or even if you have, that this training was satisfactory. Nor do I assume that you can necessarily remember what you learnt. I have met too many coaches for whom none of this was true. For instance, a colleague tells me that although she completed the training, she has never used the MBTI in her coaching because she can't see how you can get beyond what she calls 'the absurdly simplistic Type descriptions'. On investigation I discover that her training was run by a young graduate, not in the UK, who perhaps did not himself understand what he was teaching. An experienced coach to whom I act as supervisor confesses that she never consolidated her understanding of the instrument by enlisting clients immediately after her very thorough training, so she is now nervous and uncertain about how to use it. I also know innumerable coaches who use free internet versions of Jungian Type indicators with their clients but whose knowledge of the thinking behind such questionnaires has been limited to what they have been able to pick up from having been clients themselves, plus a little reading. Then there are the ones who piggy-back on to licensed practitioners, relying on them to buy the materials, hoping that their own rather more sketchy knowledge will not be exposed. One such coach mumbled embarrassedly over a glass of wine at a conference that he had only ceased doing this after he had worked with a client who turned out to know more about the questionnaire than he did.

The Preferences/Dichotomies

If you are less familiar with the special way that labels and language are used in Jungian indicators, this section is a quick reminder.

The idea of preference is crucial to understanding Jungian thinking. It is one of the main reasons why Isabel Myers' work was rejected for so long. The questionnaires are based on the idea that there are four bi-polar sets of preferences, also known as the Dichotomies because they represent psychological opposites. The assumption is that all of us can use all eight of these preferences but that we are likely to have a preference for one in each pair and that along with this preference there will probably also be comfort and skill in its use. Your preference may be anywhere on a spectrum from very slight to pronounced. Psychological health will lie in developing the upsides and managing the downsides of each preference. This was a challenge to psychometricians who favoured the idea that it was better to be in the middle – a little bit of everything – and indeed some alternative versions of Jungian questionnaires include this as a possibility.

Each of these words also has special meanings associated with it which are different from their everyday usage, so for instance, Extraversion (E) does not imply wonderful social adjustment, Intuition (N, because I has already been used for Introversion) does not mean acting on hunch, Feeling (F) does not mean being emotional and Judging (J) does not mean being judgemental. This special language of Type can be a distraction and seriously misleading. It still makes me smile when I remember a good friend, clearly an Extravert herself and with a little knowledge of the MBTI, asking me innocently if I thought her husband (INTP) and I (INTJ) were examples of 'high functioning Introverts', thus giving away her totally mistaken assumption that a preference for Introversion was somehow connected with autism.

Each of the Dichotomies has its own set of needs and associated behaviours:

Where do you get your energy?

Extraversion (E)	*Introversion (I)*
Needing action and contact with people; doing your thinking out loud; enjoying contact with people and activity; liking breadth rather than depth	Needing privacy and reflection; thinking before speaking; enjoying solitude; liking depth rather than breadth
Downsides: talking too much; not listening; exhausting yourself with too much activity	Downsides: looking cool and detached; seeming shy, under-contributing, lacking social contact

How do you perceive the world? Where does your attention go first?

Sensing (S)

Looking for tangible evidence: what you can see, taste, smell, touch, hear; detail and data; relying on what is familiar; taking things step by step

Downsides: getting too literal, resisting change

Intuition (N)

Looking for what is intangible: possibilities, ideas, patterns; the new; liking to be different; jumping in anywhere

Downsides: seeming hopelessly unpractical; over-fixed on change for its own sake

How do you make decisions?

Thinking (T)

On the basis of objectivity; standing back to see the overall; looking for what is logical and fair

Downsides: seeming tough and harsh, overlooking the personal dimension

Feeling (F)

On the basis of what is right for relationships and personal values; looking for what is compassionate

Downsides: seeming sentimental, overlooking the rational dimension

How do you live your life?

Judging (J)

Being organized and decisive; liking plans and goals

Downsides: deciding before you need to; being too serious; getting too fixed on completion

Perceiving (P)

Staying flexible and adaptable; liking to go with the flow

Downsides: missing deadlines; being too frivolous; being messy and disorganized

Choosing one from each pair of preferences produces 16 possibilities, known by the four letters of each preference.

These are thumbnail portraits of each of the 16 types:

Table 0.1 The 16 Types: thumbnail portraits

ISTJ	ISFJ	INFJ	INTJ
Thoughtful, courteous, responsible and perfectionist; needs to be in charge and wants efficiency. May feel is never off duty. Pays meticulous attention to systems and processes. Likes the clarity of sensible rules. Can be stubborn. May over-rely on detail and tend to dismiss the importance of people's feelings.	Cordial, charming, patient; modest style fuelled by wish to help others through strong sense of loyalty to duty and liking for tradition. Observant of how others feel. Detail-conscious, steady and serious; delivers on promises. May need to guard against being exploited and feeling resentful.	Sensitive, patient, insightful and hardworking; willing to put effort into understanding the complexity of human relationships. Wants to contribute decisively to ideas that will affect people in important ways in the longer term. Can be dreamy and enigmatic and may find it difficult to put self first.	Inner energy, fierce independence and a preference for big-picture thinking go with calm and unflappable public face which disguises ardour for competence - for self and others. Impatient for improvement. Likes to organize. May have air of critical detachment which creates sense of being impossible to please.

ISTP	ISFP	INFP	INTP
Socially reserved; cool observer; needs variety; can come into own when the need is for quick thinking, practicality and coping calmly with a crisis. Needs to feel can meet the unexpected with ingenuity. Detachment, need for privacy and reluctance to communicate may create problems with others.	Kind, modest, attentive to others, with little need to impress or control. Loathes conflict. Needs to give service, but on own terms. Deeply loyal with quiet sense of fun; likes to offer practical support without judging. May make an art out of economy of effort and may annoy through holding back from communicating or explaining.	Gentle, loyal and apparently pliant style may hide intensely idealistic and driven interior. Wants to live in harmony with values and expand potential of self and others. Has little interest in worldly possessions or controlling others. Endless quest for the perfect may lead to perpetual dithering or unnecessary guilt.	Analytical, sceptical, cool seeker after truth. Tends to love the complex, theoretical and novel; resists authority and dislikes being in authority; constantly challenges the status quo through experiment; always ready to re-think. May need to learn that passion for the exact truth as sees it could alienate others.

ESTP	ESFP	ENFP	ENTP
Straightforward, cheerful, inventive, practical; has zest for life and loves a challenge as long as it results in immediate tangible action. Sees self as an adaptable realist who gets round the rules. Has accepting attitude to others. Enjoys trouble-shooting. May need to take care that expediency does not dominate.	Open, modest, generous and tactful; commitment to active fun, practicality and to valuing realism about self and others. Sociable, gracious, flexible and enjoys the limelight. Relishes the good things of life without apology. May need to take care that is not seen as frivolous or unfocused.	Enthusiastic, versatile innovator. Likes to improvise and help people solve problems through creativity and insights into how people tick. Must give and receive personal authenticity. Builds bridges and 'walks the talk'. May need to guard against 'butterfly' approach which exhausts self and others.	Energetic, brash, original; wants to be where the action is. Needs to be right and to be first. Loathes routine and detail. Likes to challenge conventional wisdom and values independence. May need to beware of unintentionally hurting others through love of argument and of having the last word.
ESTJ	**ESFJ**	**ENFJ**	**ENTJ**
Crisp, decisive, courageous; wants to get things organized *now*. Needs to maintain stability and order through care with detail; has robust often hearty style with people. Down-to-earth, practical approach. May need to take care that in concern to get things done, does not overlook the need for tact and sensitivity.	Friendly, brisk, talkative, loyal and practical; brings common-sense and warmth to dealings with people. Needs approval from others. Likes busyness, organizing and socializing. Values working systematically and co-operatively. Sensitive to indifference. May need to give and take criticism in a more detached way.	Tactful, diplomatic; natural facility with words and commitment to good causes that will make a difference to the world; can inspire others. Loves encouraging others; believes passionately in equality. Sensitive to disharmony. May need to watch tendency to 'rescue' others or to allow idealism to become rigid.	Energetic, clear-sighted, decisive, analytical; needs to turn ideas into action; loathes illogicality; needs to feel authoritative. Confident and articulate. Insists on looking at the big picture and enjoys robust discussions on improving standards and implementing change. Direct style can seem abrasive and may intimidate.

The background

The Myers–Briggs Type Indicator (MBTI)®, the best known of the Jungian personality questionnaires, is the most widely used psychometric instrument in the world. Its developers, Isabel Myers and her mother Katharine Briggs, were untrained but gifted psychometric researchers whose fascination with the work of Carl Jung and belief that if there were observable patterns in nature then there would be observable patterns in human personality led them to many years of ingenious, rigorous and self-funded research. Their work is distinctively different from Jung's thinking in a number of ways, for instance in naming and labelling 'Types', something Jung himself never did, and in expanding the eight cognitive Functions that Jung identified into 16 separate Types.

After decades of scorn, dismissal and hostility, Isabel Myers' work finally gained recognition in the 1970s. The classic MBTI questionnaire is available from its US publishers, CPP, formerly Consulting Psychologists Press, distributed in the UK by OPP, formerly Oxford Psychologists Press, and available now in many languages. Today there are two versions of the questionnaire. Step I, the original, sorts you into one of the 16 Types. Step II gives a more behaviourally focused report with five sub-facets for each Dichotomy (pair of preferences) and gives considerable nuance in the scoring. But there are many other versions, for instance the Keirsey Type Indicator and the Jungian Type Indicator. On my website www.JennyRogersCoaching.com you can take a free quick version constructed so that what it measures is entirely transparent and does not purport to be anything other than an introduction to the genuine article. Chapter 3 discusses alternatives to Step I of the MBTI, all of them based to some extent on Jungian thinking.

In parallel with the work of Myers and Briggs, a thriving commercial psychometric mini-industry was also developing in the middle and later years of the twentieth century, spurred on by interest in objectively based methods of selection for jobs. This has produced many excellent questionnaires which measure a wide variety of factors including verbal reasoning, numerical ability, spatial ability, personality traits, strengths, emotional intelligence, motivation – and many more.

Interest in classifying human personality goes back into recorded history, and possibly before that to Mesopotamia or Egypt, but certainly to the Greeks where the physician Hippocrates (460–370 BC) developed his Four Temperaments theory. His explanation, that temperament was the result of different kinds of bodily fluid, now seems a little eccentric, but his descriptions of the temperaments went on being adapted and recognizably useful right up to the present day where their modern manifestation is in David Keirsey's Temperament Sorter (page 39) linked explicitly to the MBTI.

A personal history

Nearly three decades ago I was fumbling my way towards what would become my profession: coaching. At the time I knew no one else who was doing it and had no word to describe this activity – in fact, I referred to it by the vague term 'one-to-one work' after being approached for 'help' by other senior managers in the BBC. I had returned to the organization after a few years in publishing and before that was a TV producer myself. Now I was running the management development department. There was enthusiasm in my department for the MBTI, of which I had never heard.

I reluctantly enrolled myself on a two-day internal training course run by a distinguished practitioner, and then as I got to understand more about it, slowly became an enthusiast myself.

Like many others who get interested in Jungian indicators, I was green enough to believe, thanks to the two days of training I had received, that I already knew most of what there was to know and that any further training was a mere formality which would enable me to get past the irritating restrictions that would otherwise stand in the way of my buying and using the official version of the questionnaire. I booked for the five-day course run by OPP and had a shock when I realized that my knowledge was sketchy and that the end-of-course test was far from being a formality. You had to get 80% in all four papers to pass.

The exceptional rigour of this process paid off when, only 4 weeks after the training, I was introducing the questionnaire to a group of 40 young doctors, several of whom pressed me hard on the research evidence for validity. I was glad then that I could bandy T-scores and probability theory with every appearance of familiarity and comfort. Most of this, I have to say, I have now forgotten. If I did by any chance need to relearn it, I have the comprehensive technical manual to hand.

Then, like so many other coaches, I began inflicting the MBTI on my clients. What was this about? Partly it was that whenever gripped by an enthusiasm, I want to share it. Partly it was a confidence boost: remember this was at a time in the development of coaching as a profession when there was little or no coaching-specific training – we pioneers essentially had to make it up as we went along and clutch at whatever training help we could find.

Soon, I was finding a degree of resistance to the American-originated explanatory materials, excellent though I thought they were – and are. At the time they were not available in British English editions. My British clients complained that they didn't like the American tinge of the language nor understood what they called 'Type jargon' and that there was too little in these materials about leadership (this was the BBC, so the home of well-educated and therefore – how to put this politely? – sometimes over-confident and argumentatively inclined people). After more than 2 years of intensive use of the instrument with, by then, several hundred clients from a number of different organizations, I was cocky enough to believe that some further subtleties were possible. Recklessly I decided to embark on my own research project and to develop my own interpretative profiles. Fortunately by this stage I had become so gripped by the whole business of coaching that I had left the BBC in order to set up my own company so was able graciously to grant myself the time and space for this work.

Developed originally just for my own use, I set up loosely constituted criterion groups, about 15 people of each Type, and laboured over new profiles. The idea was to give clients something to read between sessions so that we could then return to their preferences at the next session. I encouraged these clients, as I still do, to highlight anything they particularly agreed with and anything that seemed plain wrong for them. Soon other coaches began requesting this material. George Davies of what was then Cambridge Management Centres, later ASK Europe, saw these profiles and liked them so we embarked on a co-publishing project which has flourished ever since with two titles, *Sixteen Personality Types at Work in Organisations* (Rogers 2007b) and *Influencing Others Using the Sixteen Personality Types* (Rogers 2007a).[2]

Why use psychometrics at all?

Coaching is a bigger topic than psychometrics and psychometrics a bigger topic than coaching. However, the meeting point is one that I find to be invaluable.

It matters to be clear in your own mind about what coaching is. The essence of coaching is that it is about change. If nothing needs to change, then you don't need a coach. The change may be that you need a new job or that you need to learn how to be a leader or how to influence others effectively or how to improve the important relationships in your life. There are dozens of definitions of coaching, many felt perhaps to be necessary because as an immature profession we have been anxious to say what it is *not*: not counselling, not consulting, not therapy, not mentoring, not psychiatry; for well people not ill people. Now after more than 30 years of success and with many thousands of coaches offering their services worldwide, perhaps we can be more confident about what we are and what we do. This is my own current definition:

> Coaching is the art of facilitating another person's learning, development, well-being and performance. Coaching raises self-awareness and identifies choices. Through coaching people are able to find their own solutions, develop their own skills and change their own attitudes and behaviours. The whole aim of coaching is to close the gap between people's potential and their current state.

It will be obvious that there is nothing in this definition about psychometrics, but it does contain the vital phrase *self-awareness*. This is where psychometric assessments have such a useful role to play, and one that I explore in detail in this book, but in truth you could be a perfectly good coach and never use a single psychometric questionnaire. After many thousands of coaching hours, I am able to put my own love affair with the MBTI into perspective. I use it with around half of my clients, so note that I don't use it with the other half. I rarely use it on its own – it normally has at least one psychometric companion (for more on this, see Chapter 10). I am clear about its weaknesses and also about its abiding strengths.

The richness of personality Type

There is no substitute for getting thorough training in whichever instrument you choose and then committing yourself to as much practice as possible, where you will for certain discover that clients do not always conform to neat rules and that human personality resists categorizing. Nonetheless I am grateful every week to all those brilliant psychometricians, including Isabel Myers and Katharine Briggs, who have made our work as coaches infinitely the richer, thanks to their insights, giving us a language and a set of systems that can add such depth to our work. In this book I make the case for using personality Type questionnaires with individuals and groups, adapting some well-known exercises and adding others that I have found to work. Since all coaching is about raising self-awareness, to do that we have to raise our own. If nothing else, work on yourself, understand your own hotspots, prejudices and strengths. Take a range of psychometrics yourself and see which ones work for you. That will always be your best guide about what will work for others.

A note on nomenclature. One of the potentially confusing aspects of psychometrics is that so many different words are used to describe them. In the US they are known as *assessments*, a word that is rarely used this way in the UK. They may also be described as *tests*, misleading if, as in the case of Jungian products, there are no right/wrong answers. Other words include *survey, indicator, instrument* and *questionnaire*. In this book I have opted for using *questionnaire* and *instrument* interchangeably.

A note on the case studies. All client details have been rigorously disguised.

Notes

1   The MBTI®, Myers–Briggs and Myers–Briggs Type Indicator are registered trademarks of the Myers and Briggs Foundation in the United States and other countries.

2   These are available from my website www.JennyRogersCoaching.com.

1 Measured enthusiasm, not evangelical fervour

A friend who is a coach is telling me wryly about a conversation she has had with her doctor brother. Wrestling with that common puzzlement about what on earth coaching is, he asks her what she actually does in a coaching session.

'I ask questions and I listen to the answers', she says coolly. He composes his face into mock amazement which is also real amazement.

'You mean people pay you money for that?'

Well yes, they do. What are they actually paying for? It cannot be that there is any obvious equivalent of the deep and specialized medical information held by a doctor and, along with it, the ability to make a difficult diagnosis which is potentially life-saving. But the answer still has to be that our clients believe we coaches have something that they cannot get from phoning a friend or a chat in the pub. The assumption is that at the very least we have wisdom, psychological sophistication, steadiness and the ability to manage our own lives well. This is why a fat coach, a heavy smoker or one whose own career has been self-sabotaged and has palpably crashed will find it harder to make a living – the plain evidence for lack of self-management will contradict claims to be able to work with others on similar issues. As coaching develops into a profession, it is clear that we also need specific and demonstrable expertise. The foundation of such expertise has surely to be our understanding of human psychology, and this is one of the ways in which personality questionnaires can add so much value.

The attractions of personality Type

The charm of getting a qualification in a personality instrument is that although it does need the money and time to invest in the training, it does not need years of experience. Having a clutch of psychometrics under your belt is a claim to expertise, useful also in adding activity streams to your practice such as doing team coaching or running development and assessment centres.

With expertise also goes confidence. Many coaches will confess to a lack of confidence because they are privately asking themselves the same question as my friend's doctor brother: why would anyone want to pay money for this? Knowing that you have expert knowledge boosts confidence. There is a less attractive side to this confidence – it may also be a lure into believing that you have power over the client. If this is the case then look it in the eye. The only way a coaching programme can work is if the coach and the client work as equals.

Psychometrics as a short cut to understanding yourself

Most of us have at least a little curiosity about ourselves: why do I always get myself into similar tangles at work? What is unique about me? Why is it that so many of my relationships seem to follow the same course? What do I really want from life? A psychometric instrument such as the MBTI gives you a crisp way of comparing yourself with others against criteria that the developers of the instrument have found will stand up to scrutiny.

The benefits of greater self-awareness are manifold: quicker and more robust decisions about career and life direction, a firmer grip on priorities, a clearer understanding of the strengths and weaknesses of your personal style, improved relationships at work and in private life, understanding that you are responsible for yourself. This is the case whether the client is a young graduate desperate for a first job or the chief executive of a FTSE/Fortune 100 company. True, clients do not generally come along to their first session saying 'I need to be more self-aware', but this is often what underlies the issues they bring:

> I've made a lot of money selling my company but now I don't know what to do with the rest of my life.

> I've been drifting round since university. I need to sort myself out but I don't have any burning ambition to be a vet or a librarian or anything else for that matter.

> It's a year since I took on the chief exec job and I'm not sure how I'm doing. I'm getting hints that the Board don't like some aspects of my style.

> There's six weeks to go before I start this big new job and I need to make sure I get myself properly ready. I don't want to repeat all my familiar mistakes.

As a coach you quickly get used to the excuses we can all give about how it's others with their pesky incompetence, infuriating brilliance, stubbornness or opaqueness that are stopping us from achieving the success we want. The truth is that you never or rarely have these annoying others in the coaching room, only your client, and in the end one of the most important questions to ask the client (and in my experience the one most coaches frequently avoid asking, though they know that they should) is 'What is your own responsibility for what's going on here?'

It no longer surprises me that clients assume that their own perceptions of how things are – and should be – is exactly like everyone else sees it. I used to do just that myself. For instance, to use a Type example, it truly amazed me when I first met the MBTI that there could be people who did not perceive the world in terms of big-picture possibilities but whose attention went first to facts and tangible data (Sensing) when my own strong preference for Intuition meant that my interest in such data was either minimal or absent. In fact for a long time I did not believe this theory to be true, it seemed so implausible – nor did I see that my own reaction was pure, if naïve, Type prejudice.

So the first and most obviously helpful use of personality Type is as a foundation for understanding yourself: there are 15 other ways of seeing life as well as an infinite number of ways in which your own Type profile can differ from those whose preferences are theoretically the same. Never under-estimate the impact this can have, especially when clients are meeting such ideas for the first time:

Kirstin (call centre manager, INFP)

I hadn't realized that all my life I'd been fighting against the idea that there was something wrong with being private and introverted. I never understood that my preference for Introversion at least partly explained my exhaustion at the end of a long day of talking, talking, talking. I don't really like being a boss and this showed me why. I'm not at all ambitious for the usual kinds of 'success'. The MBTI was a revelation as it made clear what I needed in my life in order to be happy.

When Isabel Myers wrote about the MBTI, she called her book *Gifts Differing* (1980), a biblical quote (Romans 12:6) which sums up the essence of its power. This is that no personality Type is any better or worse than any other; every Type has gifts just as every Type has blindspots. And in terms of the gifts themselves, no one gift is any more valuable than any other. The entirely radical nature of this belief is stunning in its implications. The world needs people of all Types – it is just as well, to take one example at random, that it is not peopled entirely by ENTJs as it would be full of exhausting jostling, loud argument, rival grand plans and ceaseless competition. As it is, we can be grateful that those energetic ENTJs can take their rightful place in energetically sorting out messes that would daunt other Types.

In most coaching engagements, psychometric assessments such as the MBTI take their place as one part of the process. But just occasionally the impact is the key to unlocking a whole cache of puzzling problems:

Robin (homemaker, teacher, ISFJ)

This client had been a homemaker for 20 years. At 19 she had become pregnant and had dropped out of college to marry the much older father of her baby. Now 41, with her children leaving home, she felt utterly stuck. She was divorced, she was desperate to enter the workforce and yet had little confidence. She had struggled for many years with health anxiety, a recognized mental health problem, where every small symptom, real or imagined, becomes a major illness in the mind of the sufferer. Therapeutic help had enabled her to face her fears and it was her therapist who had suggested that career coaching might be a good next step. Robin's coach debriefed the MBTI with her, establishing that Robin had developed a pattern of saying 'yes' when she meant 'no', taking on responsibilities that frightened her and then reneging on commitments at the last moment. She was an expert at passive-aggression and dressed more like a teenager than like a woman in her forties. Robin and her coach worked together on a project that Robin bravely dubbed 'becoming a real adult', identifying and then accessing the many strengths of the typical ISFJ: sensitivity, quiet support, practicality, respect for tradition, loyalty – as well as tackling the downsides which had dominated her adult life up to that point. The MBTI was pivotal here, providing insights and challenges that could not have been found so quickly or so thoroughly any other way, and these ran through all their sessions. Robin enrolled for a degree course, graduated with honours, trained as an early years teacher, remarried and is now considered to be the ultimate role model for what successful teaching means in her school.

As a coach, when you offer a client the chance to take a psychometric questionnaire you will recognize how many people back away. They are afraid: afraid that the questionnaire will reveal some inner stupidity, categorize them in ways they dislike or allow their coach to patronize them. With trait-based questionnaires such fears can be well founded. This is because a trait-based questionnaire will usually put you somewhere on a 1–10 scale suggesting how much or how little of a particular factor you have – for instance, Openness. Too much Openness may mean you are gullible, too little may mean you are suspicious and over-defended. With questionnaires based on Type principles you are being sorted into a set of preferences, not judged. You can honestly reassure clients that there is no right/wrong, better-than/worse-than. Any result is acceptable – even if clients may not always think so at first.

So at a first reading, Type profiles will reassure. This is because they are written with the best possible version of that personality Type in mind.

This may be a particular advantage with the many clients whose outer appearance of confidence is only skin deep, or with people who turn out to be the only representative of their Type in a team:

Kevin (IT consultant, INTP)

I always wondered why I felt a bit like the outsider in my department and all my life I have felt lacking in confidence – I didn't go to university and felt a bit dim by comparison with some of my friends. We did the MBTI as a team and I discovered that I was the only person in a group of 15 who had preferences for Intuition and Thinking. All the others were SFs or STs. I'd often felt irritated by their focus on what to me were petty conflicts and fussing about plant pots in the office or the insistence on celebrating everyone's birthday. I realized that my own apparent aloofness, quirky sense of humour and indifference to socializing were puzzling and alienating to my colleagues and also that I had something unique to offer to this team – essentially that it was all right to be me. My confidence began to grow from that point.

Type language has entered the bloodstream of many organizations. For instance in one global media organization, absolutely everyone in a senior management role has taken the MBTI, is fully familiar with what the preferences mean, knows the Type preferences of all their colleagues and will unselfconsciously use Type concepts in problem-solving. The same is true in several UK government departments. To be a coach to any of these people you would certainly be expected to be fully conversant with everything they talk about with such casual ease.

The simplicity of the 16-cell structure is an effective way for people to discuss differences safely, a reminder that much of other people's apparently annoying behaviour is not necessarily attributable to their doing those exasperating things on purpose but because their minds, and possibly also their brains, function differently. This is a distinct advantage in team settings: any psychometric instrument that *measures* rather than *sorts* is potentially going to be too exposing for comfort, which is why it is rare for a trait-based instrument to be used for this purpose.

Personality Type as shorthand

In the same way, the language of personality Type can become a shorthand between coach and client as the coaching programme goes on. Here is one coach, talking about the benefits:

Gwyneth (career coach, ENTP)

I administer a half-day of varied psychometrics in the early stages of any coaching programme. As we go on through the process over a period of weeks or months, I will remind the client of our discussion. So, for instance, with one finance director client, his persistence and patience with a mass of data was one of the pluses of his preference for Sensing. He was taking this for granted instead of seeing it as the gift it was, but also needed to see that his preference for Sensing and Judging was part of what made it hard for him to accept radical, sudden change. When I gathered 360 feedback for him, we also reviewed the results by drawing constantly on his Type profile – for instance that appearing to interrogate people, when in his own eyes he was merely having an ordinary discussion – was one of the ways in which an ISTJ could alarm colleagues.

In my own work I find that Type cuts through much equivocation and waffle where career coaching is the agenda. I worked recently with an ESFJ client who had to decide between two possible jobs, both seemingly equally attractive. We went back to look at what her results would suggest and discussed how far her preference for Feeling would create difficulties for her in one of the roles where conflict was clearly an everyday occurrence. In fact she went for and was offered this role. In deciding to take it, she said she felt well prepared for the psychological demands it would make, knowing that in theory it went against her strong need for harmony.

Most clients who come for executive coaching have been on the receiving end of 360 feedback questionnaires (see also page 126). Somehow, these questionnaires manage to imply that all-round perfection is possible and desirable for any manager. This contradicts everything I know about how senior leaders actually operate. They all have flaws and the idea that you can be a little bit good at everything runs the risk of smudging the impact of your actual strengths while merely raising everything else to the level of mediocrity, if that. Personality indicators are constructed differently. They assume that it is impossible to be equally good at everything and that your task is to get the maximum leverage from your gifts, leaving it to others to be good at the skills which complement yours while also doing at least a little work on your opposite preferences in due course. I find that most clients receive this idea with relief. So while, as is often rightly said, 'Type is not an excuse' for our failings, it does stop us wasting energy on a pointless quest to be geniuses in areas where we are very unlikely ever to excel.

Links with principles of coaching

I work from several firmly held principles of coaching, and these apply as much to team coaching as to individuals:

> Clients are resourceful people; they don't need 'fixing'
>
> The coach's role is to work with them to enable them to solve their own problems by creating the right environment and asking the right questions
>
> The relationship is one of equals, whatever the apparent differences in status, profession or age
>
> The client – not the coach – sets the agenda. No agenda: no coaching
>
> It is important to take a whole-life perspective including looking briefly at the past because the past is always there in the present
>
> Coaching is fundamentally about change: if clients do not wish to change, then there is no point in coaching.

All of these principles are underpinned by a belief in the principle of *choice*: we cannot be victims because we choose how we respond to the challenges that life throws at us. No one can 'make' us happy or unhappy. The role of the coach is to work with the client to make such choices explicit. Doing this means you increase the chance of making better-quality decisions and achieve it by working as respected equals. The MBTI and its Jungian rivals are the only personality-based psychometrics that I know which overtly endorse the importance of this approach to coaching. Yes, others emphasize ideas of development, equality and courtesy, but these are absolutely intrinsic to the MBTI. Yes, there are strengths-based questionnaires, but these do not claim to be about the whole personality.

When I was training to use the 16 Personality Factors (16PF) questionnaire I was the client in a practice feedback session. My would-be coach peered first at my results and then at me over his spectacles to announce, 'Hmm, I see we have an independence freak here!' This temptation to be seduced by the apparent scientific authority of all those bar or pie charts is unfortunately ever-present in so many other psychometrics. I confess that on this occasion I simply stopped listening to or taking part in what might actually have been a useful discussion because my polite mask hid furious indignation at being treated so patronizingly.

Research on the human brain shows why this is so critical. Our brains do not distinguish between a physical attack and a virtual one: the amygdala, the brain's alarm signal, sends a flood of cortisol to the prefrontal area, the seat of rationality, and the cortisol shuts down the brain's higher thinking processes. Unwanted or clumsily given advice is treated by the brain as an attack, just as certainly as it did when our Stone Age ancestors were facing a predator or a human enemy and therefore the brain prepares us to run away by sending oxygen and glucose to the rest of the body.

Consultation, collaboration, respectful discussion and encouraging the client to have the last word are all built into Jungian instruments and the debrief/feedback discussion (see Chapter 4) is structured to ensure that this is what happens. For this reason alone, they are special.

It's not all pluses

For all their manifest attractions, there are disadvantages associated with using personality Type indicators. The first is that you will find many people who claim to have 'done' the questionnaire before. The MBTI is so very well known that when you mention it to clients they may be privately thinking that you are merely re-treading territory that they have already covered and that your coaching will therefore lack surprise, freshness and originality.

All personality Type practitioners hate the 'H' word – horoscope. This is the downside of the sunny uplands of positivity in which Type profiles appear to be bathed. 'Oh yes, it's just like a horoscope!' cries the client. Unlike research into psychological Type, no scientific study has ever been able to prove that there is any validity whatsoever in astrology. The happy glow apparently present in the MBTI can be countered to some extent by the material in any decent Type profile which points out that each Type has blindspots as well as strengths. However, the amount of space given to blindspots is almost always considerably less than that given to strengths. There is help on how to deal with both these issues in Chapter 5.

The Barnum effect

Then there is the Barnum effect. Phineas Barnum was a nineteenth-century showman and hoaxer who took scornful pleasure in sneering at the credulity of his customers, though he never did utter the phrase attributed to him, 'One sucker born every minute'. The relevance to psychometric profiles is the well-known experiment in which people took a questionnaire and were then shown the allegedly uniquely created results. Many vowed that it was 100% accurate about their personality. In fact all the subjects in the experiment had been given identically worded profiles, a perfect example of 'cold reading' – the process by which necromancers, astrologers, mediums, palm-readers and others in the same genre have deceived their customers with phrases which could apply to everyone such as 'You can be extraverted when you need to be but you can also be reserved' or 'You enjoy taking the lead when the circumstances are right, but can be prone to self-doubt on occasions'.

My own experience is that exploring the less comfortable aspects of personality is an essential part of the coach's duty, and after supervising many hundreds of trainee coaches and listening to their recorded sessions, I know that any kind of challenge is the very thing that almost every beginner coach finds troubling. A coaching conversation is unlike most other conversations in that there is licence to challenge as much as to support, but the challenging has to be done with extreme care, which is perhaps why so many coaches back away from it. So the only true way around the Barnum effect is to do a proper feedback and interpretation session (Chapter 4). How well this goes will depend critically on the skill of the coach – and not every coach can carry this off.

At the introductory level, the Type profiles are easy to absorb and remember, but this strength is also a weakness as it can lead to the unthinking accusation that the profiles label and restrict, or that it is absurd to believe that there are only 16 ways to be in the world – as indeed it would be, if this were what the MBTI is about. The fact that the MBTI Type table is presented as a grid with 16 cells is an unfortunate visual reinforcement of this idea. If practitioners really believed that the 16 core profiles represented everything that can be said about any individual, then of course this accusation would be fair and it is why you need to handle the feedback session honestly and skilfully so that such misconceptions are safely defused.

Theoretical complexity

Another potential weakness of personality Type questionnaires is the theoretical complexity, related to Jungian thinking, that lies behind the apparently bland and simple exterior. According to the senior practitioners who write so well about Type, to get beyond the beguiling ease of the four-letter profiles is to get into what is often described as 'the real richness' of these instruments. But I have lost count of how many times other MBTI practitioners have guiltily and privately enquired whether I go into Type dynamics or Type development with my clients. It is obvious from the question that these coaches baulk at the task and the fact that they do so is extremely understandable.

On the BBC training course where I first met the instrument, our tutor patiently described the principles and 'rules' of Dominant, Auxiliary, Tertiary and Inferior Functions (see page 56). She explained them more than once and in several different ways. At the time I believed I was the only person in the room who had not understood what on earth she was talking about, though I later discovered this to be untrue. The fact is that the formula is difficult to follow and I have found that clients' eyes mostly glaze over when I try to explain it.

Hostility in the early years of development

From its inception, the MBTI attracted criticism. When Isabel Myers was fighting to have her work taken seriously in the 1950s and 1960s her difficulties were compounded by her gender and by the taken-for-granted sexism of the time: one of her critics described her as 'a little old lady in tennis shoes'. They enjoyed pointing out that she was not a trained statistician, nor a licensed psychologist, and some of the criticisms of her work had, and still have, the flavour of resentment at an intruder: how dare she make these claims when she was merely a woman, apparently just a hobbyist interested in psychometrics? Isabel Myers' own behaviour was often labelled 'difficult' in a way that similar behaviour from a man would not be. It was said that staff at her then publisher (Educational Testing Service) asked for the day off when she came to Princeton or tried to hide because she was so demanding. The massive quantity and quality of longitudinal research she had undertaken was dismissed because she had done so much of it under her own aegis rather than as a conventional academic project. The impetus in psychometric research at the time was in trait-based instruments, as it still is, and the dichotomous structure of the MBTI was judged to be quirky and eccentric by contrast.

Attacks on the MBTI have commonly focused on its alleged weaknesses. Some critics appear to have misunderstood the idea of preference, assuming that it means, for instance, that if you report as someone with a preference for Introversion this means you can never do Extraverted behaviour, whereas it has always been a firmly held principle of the MBTI that all of us can call on behaviour associated with all eight of the preferences, but at heart are likely to prefer one over the others as our default. This may be too subtle, or as one such psychologist critic once said to me, 'too vague and wiffly-waffly', for some people.

Scientific controversy

It is true that there have been thousands of studies but not all of them are flattering or support some of the MBTI's theoretical pillars, and critics point out that many have been carried out under the auspices of the Centre for Applications of Psychological Type (CAPT), which is wholly owned by CPP, the publishers of the MBTI. If you are going to use psychological Type questionnaires you need to be aware that from their inception with the MBTI, personality Type indicators have attracted controversy.

A normal distribution?

The bi-modal structure of the MBTI (two possibilities for each dimension, with a clear midpoint) should show a bi-modal distribution (Figure 1.1), but many studies show a normal (bell-shaped) curve (Figure 1.2), suggesting that many of us cluster in the middle (or mean) area as we do in other tests. If Type theory held up, that there is a clear midpoint which is the cut-off between one preference and another, then studies of large populations would show that each half

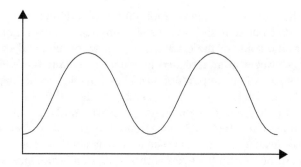

Figure 1.1 Bi-modal distribution curve

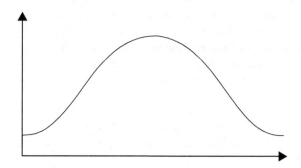

Figure 1.2 Normal distribution curve

of, say, Extraversion and Introversion has its own hump in the middle. This does not seem to be the case.

The claims of the publishers for test–retest reliability have been challenged by those researchers whose own results have shown that when people take the questionnaire again, they will report with different results more frequently than is required for validity. There is also plenty of evidence, probably from more scrupulously designed studies, showing that the MBTI does as well or better in this respect – and my own experience certainly supports this.

Unlike many trait-based instruments, most Type questionnaires are transparent and do not have mechanisms for spotting people who deliberately falsify their results (known as 'faking good' and 'faking bad'). Especially if you have taken the instrument previously, it is obvious which questions measure which dimension. This transparency encourages second guessing. So where a client feels, rightly or wrongly, that a particular Type is valued in their organization, this can lead to faking. It is also easy to produce a result which is how you would ideally like to be because you undervalue the characteristic behaviour which goes with your actual and natural Type preferences.

There is particular controversy over theories of Type dynamics (page 56), with some psychometricians claiming that the research for the validity of the theories is largely based on anecdote. To read a 2009 paper, published by CAPT, and which comprehensively attempts to demolish the theory, see https://www. capt.org/research/article/JPT_Vol69_0109.pdf.

Journalistic attacks

I notice that once every three years or so, a respected popular journal contains a long-form article on the MBTI. These pieces are rarely complimentary and the criticisms are mirrors of those made by hostile psychometricians. For an example see this article from the *Financial Times*: http://on.ft.com/2i8qnSI. If you are relatively new to the whole world of Jungian Type you may well have been dismayed by such articles: have you been duped? Is your enthusiasm misplaced? Is the whole thing a non-scientific confidence trick?

To put this into context you have to understand how journalists operate. I do understand this. I have been a freelance journalist and have made documentary films myself. I have worked extensively with journalists as coaching clients, including some very senior people such as editors of high-profile TV or radio programmes and national newspapers. The best journalists are natural sceptics. They are often solo operators who resist being 'managed'. The idea of self-development can be intrinsically absurd to such people: it makes them think of ludicrous gurus who get rich by preaching daft platitudes to credulous people. They resist the idea that anything as complex as human personality can be reduced to 'Types'. They will tell you that *psychobabble* or *management-speak* of any kind brings them out in spots. The frame of mind in which an individual journalist starts their research is often 'These people are charlatans and it is my mission to expose them'.

In writing about the origins of the MBTI, many journalists have been unable to resist describing Isabel Myers and her mother as 'housewives'. There can be a sneering tone to these articles where the overtly cynical journalist describes taking the 'test' themselves, with no motivation other than to get their piece written, then denounces the results as banal. Often these articles are strongly held opinion masquerading as balanced reporting. It would be rare to advise readers to make up their own minds: the temptation to pronounce is overwhelming.

Research evidence

Overall there is a mass of research which does indeed support much of the thinking behind the MBTI. For instance, the development of the 'Big Five' personality questionnaires (page 135), an exercise in bringing together much research into trait-based instruments, shows considerable overlap with the

MBTI categories: the only one not appearing in the Big Five category is the one which measures emotional stability (Neuroticism), something that the MBTI is expressly designed not to assess.

You will come to your own conclusions on all of this. I find that most of the assertions of the original Jungian thinking largely hold up in practice as long as I am able to honour one of the basic ethical principles: that the client is always the best judge of the accuracy of any results. And to remember that there is no one personality instrument which can tell everything about a human being, nor is there ever likely to be.

Evangelical fervour

Uniquely among psychometrics, the MBTI and other personality Type instruments attract evangelism. There is something about them that can lure practitioners into losing their sense of proportion. Perhaps this is because it does have overtly Christian reference points with its emphasis on each person having 'gifts differing', its unambiguously tolerant approach to psychological difference and its emphasis on the importance of the client having the last word. The MBTI itself has also been taken up with enthusiasm by Christian groups, so you can buy books on the MBTI with explicitly spiritual dimensions. It is impossible and a little comical to imagine other instruments having books on prayer, meditation or faith. This, like any other expression of fervour, can be off-putting to those who do not share it.

So however passionate you are about the MBTI, beware of seeming to want to convert your client into joining some kind of cult. Enthusiasm in itself is attractive; narrowly focused evangelism which ignores sensible criticism or the use of other instruments and approaches is not.

Summary

All of the leading psychometric questionnaires have strengths and matching weaknesses. This is as true of the MBTI and other Jungian instruments as of any of their rivals. Their attraction is their instantly appealing simplicity and the positive spin they put on human behaviour. Some aspects of Jungian theory are complex and have been disputed by other psychometricians. Conversely, another weakness is that they may appear too bland: it is largely up to the client, and maybe his or her persistent and tactful coach, to measure how far the promise of a Type profile is fulfilled in practice – and that, of course, is where it gets interesting.

2 Being clear about purpose and ethics

Many people who are new to coaching start with a degree of blithe confidence. Perhaps they have had an excellent coach themselves and if so, this will be someone – as with all skilled professionals – who makes it look easy. The effortless way their coach worked has hoodwinked the beginner into believing that coaching is simple. It often comes as a shock to find out that it is not. In the training courses I run myself I feel it is a good outcome if by the end of the first tranche of learning, the beginner coach has a degree of prudent confidence and is also acutely aware of what they don't know. It is often at this stage that the cry goes up, 'I need more tools and techniques!'

Partly this happens because it is a respectful nod to the necessity of broadening your personal range and a recognition that other coaches have developed ingenious ways of dealing with all the typical problems that clients bring. It is certainly helpful to have a wide range of possible approaches tucked away in your head, even if you rarely use them. Not least it is a reminder that any coaching session is improved by changes of pace, by introducing variations in tone and mood and by having playful and serious moments.

The downside is that clients can quickly spot a 'technique' and may not feel as wholehearted as you about its use. Having coached several of what I dub 'coaching divorcees', people who have already had and discarded one coach, I have found that what unites them all is that they were rapidly aware that the coach was over-dependent on what one called *tricks*:

> Whenever the coaching seemed to be running out of steam, she would say, 'Let's do some visioning!'

> My coach had been on what I later discovered was a Neuro-Linguistic Programming (NLP) course, and for the next two sessions, until I stopped him, he insisted on trying to get a 'parts conversation' going. This was apparently where one part of my mind needed to talk to another part. I thought it was ridiculous.

> I went to a counsellor after losing my job because I was so distressed, and all she did was repeat my words to me. I discovered later this was called 'reflecting back'. I felt I might just as well have talked to myself in a mirror – and saved myself a lot of money, so I stopped going.

Beware of letting it seem as if psychometric instruments fall into the same category.

Introducing psychometrics for the right reasons

In deciding whether it is appropriate to use a personality Type instrument, you need to align three separate interests: your own, the client's and those of the client's organization (if you are doing executive coaching).

The coach's interests

Coaching only works when it is a conversation between equals. This means that although the client may have accomplishments and skills in their world, you are confident in your own matching levels of skill as a coach. This is a big ask. We coaches are as affected as anyone else by the way the world regards our clients. You may be secretly in awe of your client if they are famous in their field, older than you or have attained a higher level of seniority than you did in your own earlier career. It can work the other way too, when you are coaching someone younger or relatively junior. A 'technique' can boost your confidence. When you are nervous and insecure about how good you are as a coach, or know that you are inexperienced, and that perhaps the client knows or can spot this, a 'technique' can feel like a buttress. Where you are a little overconfident because the client seems young and nervous, there can be a temptation to dominate with your wisdom.

This is especially true where psychometrics are concerned. You have done the training and know the instrument, you know its secrets and what it can reveal. Best of all, you know that debriefing a psychometric can easily take up a whole session, so you are not facing the dread that can come with insisting that the client sets the agenda, one of the main principles of coaching, and one that can leave you with the queasy feeling that you cannot do much in the way of preparation for that session because you have no idea what the client will bring to you. A 'technique' puts you in control. It postpones the moment where it is just you and the client and you have to decide what questions to ask – without the benefit of props.

In working over the years, and now with many thousands of hours of coaching experience, I have met only a handful of clients who have actually asked me to administer a psychometric as part of the coaching. The rest of the time it has been my suggestion, so in effect I am setting the agenda at least for that session, thus altering the balance of power, and altering it even more during the debrief where I have the knowledge of the construction and purpose of the questionnaire and the client does not. I have also met coaches who confess to a frisson of pleasure when a client tells them, in advance of the debrief session, of their fears about what the results may mean.

One of the core ethical principles of coaching, as in any other profession, is to operate within the boundaries of your competence. It is not ethical to offer a client a questionnaire where you do not have appropriate training and experience: the chances are that you will misrepresent the questionnaire or misinterpret the results. Lack of in-depth knowledge will also quickly become apparent to the client. Several of my own clients have recounted examples of inappropriate debriefing from coaches who were clearly not licensed practitioners, or if they were, had forgotten everything they had learnt during their training:

> The coach squabbled with me when I said that the profile did not seem at all like me, telling me that I was 'in denial'.

> I asked a few mild questions about how the MBTI was constructed and she seemed embarrassed because she could not reply – just mumbled something and moved quickly on.

> He confessed that he'd never done the training but had picked it up as he went along. This became obvious as the conversation continued as he could not answer any of my questions, just kept referring to the printout of the profile.

The lesson here is that it is essential to do the training and to keep up to date with the most recent research on whichever instrument you use. I was reminded of this only a few weeks ago. I was running a supervision session for a new client-coach who was unaware of my interest in the MBTI. He is a chartered psychologist with a visceral dislike for what he called 'Carl Jung and all his slippery nonsense'. When the inevitable subject of using psychometrics in coaching came up, we were able to have an affable peer–peer conversation about current research evidence on the MBTI along with an equally measured conversation about other instruments – and to agree to differ.

The client's needs

My own policy is never to assume that I will use any psychometric instrument as a matter of routine. It is always open to negotiation and judgement. The question here is not whether it will be good for me, but whether it will be in the client's declared and best interests.

A few years ago I answered a phone call from someone who announced herself as a human resources advisor for a large healthcare organization. She said she was looking for someone to do a debrief on the MBTI.

'You mean as part of a coaching programme?'

'No', she said, 'it's just a single session'.

She then went on to say that not only was she looking for someone to run this one-off session but she was inviting me to put myself on a list of people who would tender for the work. *Tendering* for a single two-hour session? I stifled my incredulity at this preposterous waste of public money and politely said it was not for me – and explained why.

I suggest that you never agree to do a freestanding debriefing session. Such sessions will be untethered, floating in some never-never land of unspoken or just vague aims. You will not be able to follow up and are unlikely to be able to offer any psychometric results within anything that matters to the client or the organization.

Instead, look for the opportunity to use such instruments as part of a longer programme of some sort, perhaps as a coaching follow-up to a management development programme or as part of a coaching programme of your own. The shorter the coaching programme, the more you should ask whether psychometrics justify the time they will take. So, for instance, if the organization is limiting the coaching to $4\frac{1}{2}$ hours (three 90-minute sessions), then introducing psychometrics could easily take up a third of the available time. There may be circumstances where this is legitimate, but be clear what value they will add before agreeing.

You should be able to make a convincing case to the client about the advantages of investing the amount of time and effort involved in taking any psychometric questionnaire. Do this by making explicit links with the overall agreed aims of the coaching programme – for instance clarity about career, improving relationships with colleagues, developing more emotional intelligence, leadership style and skills. If you cannot make such links, then other approaches will be better.

If it is not clear what the benefits would be, or if the client resists, then drop the idea. If you still sincerely believe that there are likely to be major gains for the client but you are getting resistance, then it may be worth making some further attempts at persuasion:

Maxine (coach, ENFJ)

My work is all with very senior people who have been made redundant. There is usually reasonably generous funding, so time is not the issue. I had one client, an ESTJ, who I believe felt deep-down that I would somehow be able to see into his soul if we did what he persisted in calling 'tests'. His self-esteem had been very bruised by losing his job but he hid behind a lot of bluster. I am always prepared to work with the grain of what the client wants, but in this case I felt it would be restorative for him to take the MBTI in particular as it would enable him to get an objective view of his strengths. So I asked his permission to make the case again – and this time I must have been more persuasive, as he agreed. That was actually the turning point as his confidence palpably began to recover from that session on.

Some clients may not gain much benefit from taking a personality Type questionnaire:

Tristram (civil engineer, most probably ESTP)

Tristram was working for a construction company when he came to me for coaching where the focus was to be on whether or not to compete for a more senior managerial role. He described himself as 'a hands-on, roll-up-your-sleeves engineer'. He had a nice line in brightly coloured shirts, a deep, confident voice and cheerfully told me that people sometimes took against him at first because they saw him as 'an over-privileged posh boy', though as he said, smiling, 'I soon tell them this is class prejudice and they should judge me on my work not my accent'. He told me readily that his liking for talking could get out of hand, that he thought he might be 'a bit lacking in the EQ department', was devoted to his hobby, rebuilding classic cars and then competing in rallies, and that his high-energy approach to life and work could be overpowering. At the same time he was well aware of all the pluses of each of these characteristics. He had taken full advantage of the 360 feedback offered by his company, telling me that it had contained no surprises. Since our coaching was strictly limited to three 2-hour sessions, I felt that personality Type questionnaires were unlikely to offer much in the way of further enlightenment. In discussing the pros and cons with him, we quickly concluded that there were better uses of our time.

Never agree to use a personality Type instrument where there has been any whiff of coercion. Taking it must be voluntary as its purpose is personal development and no one can or should insist on the personal development of another, whether this is through the use of a psychometric or any other tool.

Nor is such coercion likely to be successful as it will merely result in a sulky and resistant client or one who makes sure that the results are sabotaged:

Duncan (senior manager, utilities company, INTJ)

We were informed that everyone 'had' to take the MBTI because 'we need to know who we have at senior levels'. I thought this was sinister and so did most of my colleagues. I asked what would happen to the results and was told we would all get a print out from the online administration. That was it. Someone in our team had taken it before and told us how it was constructed. We agreed we would all make sure our results reflected ENTP. As a tactic this must have been successful as this was the last we ever heard of the MBTI!

Inappropriate use of specialist knowledge

When you qualify to use a personality Type instrument you are asked to subscribe to a code of ethics. This will include a moral obligation never to use such instruments for selection, agreeing that they cannot say anything about intelligence or aptitude, promising never to misrepresent your own levels of competence and experience, and knowing that you have to be aware at all times of your own Type biases. These principles can seem easy to endorse. In practice I have often seen them flouted. The most serious of these breaches can be hard to spot. For instance, they can involve using your own knowledge of the instrument to create a fog of subtle criticism of a colleague or client. Listening to a recorded session from a trainee coach who was debriefing the MBTI with her client, I heard the coach make a swingeing generalization about a colleague with whom her client had a troubled relationship, colluding with her client by saying, 'Of course, as an ISTJ he will be obsessed with fussy detail and pointless processes.' This coach had never met her client's colleague. All she knew was that the colleague had reported as ISTJ during a team awayday.

A client I will call John had to deal with a multi-layered and difficult disciplinary problem. John's boss was called in to adjudicate. In briefing himself, the boss asked the department's HR advisor for a view on the matter. Instead of commenting verbally, informally and judiciously, this advisor, a licensed MBTI practitioner, wrote a report which he copied to many other senior people. It contained phrases such as 'John has a preference for Thinking rather than Feeling which may explain his lack of people skills'. Then, later in the same report, 'John has a personality preference for Judging and this will be linked to his practice of closing down a discussion too soon'. I had no view myself on how well or badly John had dealt with the original question, but even now, many years later, I can still feel a stab of horror at what I read when John sent this document to me. This kind of lofty certainty – and its duplicitous and vengeful verdict on another person – is an appalling breach of ethical principles. It is the direct opposite of the nuanced and subtle understanding that the MBTI offers on human behaviour.

The organization's needs and interests

In every executive coaching engagement there are three partners: the coach, the client and the organization. Using a psychometric instrument should fit into whatever broad aims the organization has for its staff member. Ideally there should be 'three-cornered contracting', an open process where coach, client and line manager meet together to discuss the overall aims of the coaching and how any outcomes will be measured. Normally the coach asks for and facilitates this meeting. Raise the question of psychometrics at this point. Some organizations may insist that any potential coach holds a licence to administer their favourite questionnaires on the sensible grounds of consistency.

Very occasionally I hear of organizations which have used personality Type instruments as part of an assessment centre, in other words for selection. This will give a meaningless result that is beyond just unethical. A personality Type instrument is not designed to tell you whether any individual has skill, intelligence or maturity. It cannot measure adjustment or stability. So you could be an INFP with all the downsides of that Type preference: constantly engaging in a pointless quest for perfection in relationships, touchy, unconfident, disorganized. Or you could be an INFP with all the upsides: a good listener, modest, non-judgemental, insightful and loyal to your inner circle of devoted friends. It is also perfectly possible to display all the upsides as well as all the downsides. Just knowing the reported Type of an INFP will not tell you where any individual is on that spectrum. If you are asked to run such an exercise, refuse.

Knowing that the purpose is selection will also lead participants to second-guess about whichever Type they believe, rightly or wrongly, the organization is seeking to appoint, leading to flawed results.

Making your ethical principles clear

I make it clear that I will not disclose psychometric data any more than I would disclose other confidential material from the coaching, saying that the client may say whatever they wish about it, but I cannot. With one client organization whose HR person indignantly challenged me with the words 'But we're paying you', I had to explain that disclosure instantly destroys trust between coach and client and that if they wanted me to do an *assessment* of the client I would be happy to do so but this would be a different process and one that would be set up with the full knowledge of the client that this was its purpose.

Where an organization asks for some kind of mass administration, ask what purpose this is designed to serve and ideally knit yourself into whatever this is. For instance, I would agree to be part of the faculty where an organization has designed an ambitious leadership development programme and wants to ensure that each participant has an individual MBTI debrief during it. I have refused such invitations where I have merely been asked as a licensed practitioner to supply the materials with no say in or control over how the results will be used, and have also refused where the commissioning organization has remained vague about what it expects to get out of its investment.

It is also worth asking where any results will be stored and what safeguards there are against them being used at some time in the future for a different purpose. For instance, it would be unethical to encourage people to take part in a personality Type exercise which is pitched as a development exercise only to use the results later as part of a forced redundancy programme.

Finally, beware of using any personality Type instrument as the sole psychometric. Blend it with others where you can; this is the focus of Chapter 10.

Summary

Ethical use of psychometrics matters. Participation should be voluntary, everyone involved should be clear what the purpose is and should get skilled feedback from a trained practitioner, and the purpose should match the stated aims of the instrument. Always work within the boundaries of your own competence and do not hesitate to refuse to administer any instrument if you suspect that taking part could breach your own values.

3 Which questionnaire?

There are many Jungian questionnaires now on the market. In this chapter I look at how to choose the questionnaire best suited to your purpose. Even if you are devoted to the MBTI original, as I am, it is useful to know what the alternatives are. You may find that at least one of these offers you something valuable. Also you may work with clients who have adopted one of the variants and you will need to know what its advantages and disadvantages are compared to the MBTI.

The MBTI: victim of its own popularity

The MBTI, the original Type questionnaire, has been in existence one way or another for nearly eight decades. Its current publishers, CPP, have understandably held tightly to their copyright and distribution rights. To buy the questionnaire you need to be a licensed user and to be a licensed user you need to have undertaken a training programme approved by the publishers. If you don't get through the exam at the end of the course you cannot buy it. By insisting on this, the publishers are applying quality control to protect their brand and doing what any sensible brand tries to do, which is to point to its specialness. If a brand is not special, then technically it becomes a *commodity*, something such as a throwaway ball-point pen that you will buy at the cheapest possible price. The publishers are a business and they need to generate profits, at least some of which will be ploughed back into further research and development. This strategy has proved highly successful: the MBTI has been updated frequently, has been translated into many languages and millions of people take it every year.

Its very success has made the MBTI astonishingly visible, but visibility attracts competition and attention, some of it hostile.

Because of its dominance in the world of psychometric assessment, the MBTI is the subject of far more scrutiny than any of its rivals. Some articles, for instance, compare it unfavourably with 'Big Five' questionnaires without subjecting any of the available Big Five questionnaires (page 135) such as the NEO to the same intense levels of analysis, leading me to conclude that higher standards of proof are asked of the MBTI than for any of its competitors. So, for instance, Big Five questionnaires are sometimes described as being 'objective' in a way that the MBTI is not, yet each of the dimensions on these questionnaires is obviously value-laden. Ask yourself, would you really like to be described as the opposites of Open, Conscientious or Agreeable? And how pleasant is it to be labelled Neurotic?

The emergence of other Jungian instruments

The commercial successes of the MBTI and the kinds of criticisms I discuss above and in Chapter 1 have inevitably created competitors. Most such competitors have returned to Carl Jung's theories and, since there is no copyright in ideas, have been able to put their own twist on them, sometimes claiming that they are closer to Jungian 'truth' than the MBTI. Some of these competing instruments have had generous amounts of investment and the research behind the best of them is impressive.

Most of these substantial rivals have consciously sought to address common criticisms of the MBTI. Here are some of the ways in which you might see the differences:

- Avoiding the 16-cell table because of the way it appears to box and stereotype; presenting findings as a circle, pie chart, mandala, star or through using the names of colours
- Ignoring any references to the more complex aspects of Jungian Type such as Type dynamics and Type development; simplifying the theory
- Developing trait-based versions of Jungian thinking where it is possible to be at the midpoint without being accused of 'inconsistency'
- Addressing the criticism that the MBTI is 'too positive' by offering alternative versions of an individual's personality – for instance what happens at your best compared with what happens under stress. Or these alternatives may offer an 'external' and an 'internal' or at work/ at home personality description
- Many have developed software which enables unique individual interpretations to be made, including self-reported behaviour which is seemingly at odds with the conventional picture of that Type
- Offering the variant of asking colleagues to fill in a questionnaire about you to challenge any delusions you might have about how your behaviour strikes others
- Reducing the number of possibilities from 16 to four, making it easier to remember the categories

- Avoiding word-pair items on the grounds that these are freighted with social meanings and therefore difficult to translate into other languages – and may not be meaningful even in different English-speaking countries
- Designing a questionnaire without forced-choice (ipsative) items and asking respondents to assess their behaviour on a five-point scale where a middle choice is possible
- Avoiding the MBTI's special language (for instance *Sensing, Judging*), all of which has to be 'explained' as the words have different meanings from their everyday use: finding simpler words with less ambiguous meanings
- Aiming explicitly at the leadership and organizational market
- Combining Jungian thinking with other lenses for looking at personality such as Belbin Team Roles or the DISC questionnaires
- Pricing their products competitively.

Step II of the MBTI

CPP, the publishers of the MBTI, have responded to many of these criticisms themselves by producing a constantly updated Step II version of the MBTI, so in comparing the MBTI with competitors you need to be clear which version you have in mind. Step II of the MBTI does in fact have many of the same advantages as the rival Jungian instruments I describe below.

Step II adds considerable subtlety to Step I. The questionnaire has additional items and breaks each of the four Dichotomies/preferences into five further 'facets' each with two opposite poles (Figure 3.1).

The facets may help, for instance, when clients consider their results on Thinking and Feeling (Figure 3.2). So a mature senior manager could have a clear preference for Thinking as the basis for decision-making, able to make difficult decisions on the basis of fairness and logic, unafraid of asking tough questions, yet score what is known as 'out of preference' on Compassionate and Tender because they have a well-developed ability to see how their decisions might impact on other people. The feedback discussion here can reinforce strengths as well as raising questions about how effectively the client is using all the facets.

Step II allows for considerable individual variation and may be particularly beneficial for people who are uncertain of their 'best-fit' Type as well as helping clients to understand that how they personally express their preferences will contain much that is nuanced and unique to them:

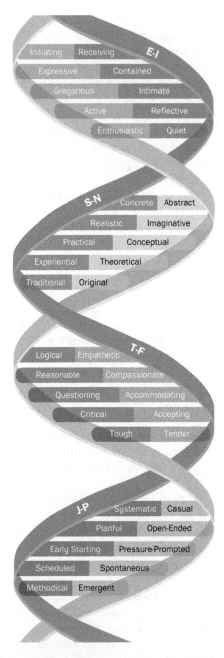

Figure 3.1 The facets associated with each of the preferences from Step II of the MBTI

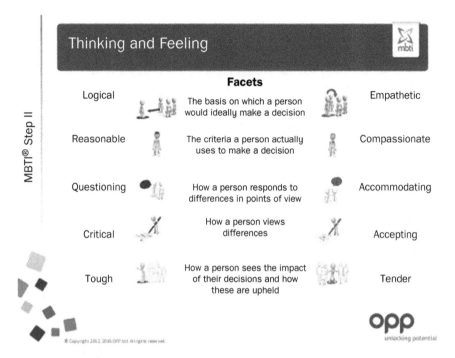

Figure 3.2 The Thinking and Feeling facets of Step II of the MBTI

Source: Copyright 2015 OPP Ltd. Reproduced with the permission of OPP, Oxford, England. All rights reserved.

Aleksandr (actor, INFJ)

Aleksandr, a gifted actor, was wondering whether he should make a career change. Stage, film and TV parts were hard to come by in an overcrowded profession, though he was doing reasonably well, despite struggling for some years with anxiety about live performances. Reporting on Step I with a preference for Introversion, Aleksandr was initially resistant to the idea that this could be his preference. 'I'm an actor', he said, 'I like performing!' But it was clear in our debrief discussion that he also liked and needed privacy and that the stage fright he suffered in the theatre was a direct result of feeling that so many pairs of eyes were, as he put it, 'staring' at him. Introversion was definitely his preference.

Step II was a revelation. Yes, he scored exactly as you would expect with mid-zone or clear preferences for Quiet, Receiving and Reflective, but had scores for 'out of preference', in other words more as an E might behave, on *Gregarious* and *Expressive*. This made perfect sense to him. His deep love for and close study of classic theatre texts (Shakespeare, Chekov, Ibsen) had, as he put it, 'liberated the actor' in him, enabling him to learn the value of being *expressive* and *gregarious*. During our coaching Aleksandr decided to give up the hunt for stage work and turned instead to corporate role-playing, for which, it turned out, he had considerable talent. The small-scale, intimate environment suited him while also allowing him to use his many talents as an actor.

Questions to ask about other Jungian instruments

In considering alternatives to the MBTI, there are some general questions to consider first. A personality questionnaire is just one type of psychometric. There are others, for instance, that measure verbal reasoning, motivation or psychological strengths. All psychometric questionnaires should adhere to the classic principles which govern their quality:

> *Reliability*: the instrument is consistent in the results it gives over time and when it is administered to the same person at a later date
> *Validity*: the instrument measures what it claims to measure
> *Standardization*: the instrument has been designed objectively and consistently
> *Freedom from bias*: the instrument produces the same results regardless of culture, nationality, gender, age.

Here are some questions to ask yourself about specific instruments:

What do the publishers say about the underlying theory, assumptions (construct) and research? How sensible does this seem to you? How do they acknowledge their debts to Jung and Isabel Myers? Look carefully at what the publishers say about the research behind their questionnaire. For how long has it been in development? How often has it been updated? What size is the norm group?

Has it been peer-reviewed? Look for a place where the instrument has been subjected to review in a respected academic journal. If you are not a psychometrician yourself, and few of us are, you will need to rely on specialists to raise the awkward questions, for instance about the size of the norm group or test–retest reliability.

Who do you know who uses it? What feedback do they report from their clients? Why do they say they prefer this questionnaire to the classic MBTI?

Probe the reasons in depth, for instance about the nature of their clients and why they believe the alternative to the MBTI to be a better match. So, for instance, you may find that some coaches like the simplicity of products which are based on four colours and which produce short, simply written reports. Coaches who frequently run workshops may find that they like systems which offer attractive ways to work with teams.

How well does this questionnaire fit with your own coaching 'offer'? Are your clients likely to agree readily to taking it, and if so, how are they likely to feel about the results?

What do the publishers say about their target market? Some try to appeal to a general market, some more consciously aim for the managerial and leadership market and their reports make reference to common managerial dilemmas about delegating and giving feedback. Some, aiming for student populations, have a focus on learning and development; their reports emphasize differences in learning style. It is tricky to create a report which covers all of these disparate needs and publishers may offer different versions of the questionnaire for different target populations.

What training do the publishers offer? What does the training course cost? How long is it? How is it structured? Some publishers make it easy to add their licensing to your existing psychometric qualifications by offering short 'bridging', 'conversion' or 'top-up' courses at low cost, so it is worth asking if this is the case for any questionnaire in which you are interested. How long would it take you to recoup the investment in time and money that you have made in the training? Is there a formal assessment of skill and knowledge at the end of the training or can you get qualified simply by attending? A participant who fails such a test and does not take advantage of the offer to resit will never buy the materials, so this represents a lost commercial opportunity. Some publishers hesitate to apply pass/fail end-of-course tests because they fear the anger of people who have spent good money on the course and will, they think, resent being told they have failed to reach the standard.

Does this questionnaire give you a competitive advantage? This is a more complicated question than it may seem. It is no longer a competitive advantage to be licensed to use the MBTI because it is so commonly deployed in the coaching community, but it may be a disadvantage not to have it when so many organizations are enthusiasts for it and may expect you to be fluent in understanding it. On the other hand, offering something different may be intriguing to clients, especially if they have expressed scepticism about the MBTI.

What does the test cost per administration? If it is high, how likely are you to meet price resistance from your clients, assuming that you will expect them to cover such costs? If you include these costs, what proportion of your fee does this leave? Alternatively, can you add a reasonable mark-up to the cost of buying it? Does the publisher offer discounts for administering the questionnaire in bulk?

What different versions of the questionnaire are available? Some publishers offer short introductory versions at a low price with further options available to cover topics such as leadership style or responses to stress. Some will still offer paper as well as online versions, and there are many situations where this will be useful.

If the questionnaire has been translated into your own language from English, how do you rate the translation? Has the translated version been subjected to the same scientific rigour as the original? What is the quality of the reports – for instance, do they read as if they have been written by a native speaker?

What back-up materials are available? With the MBTI there is a comprehensive manual for practitioners, an extensive library of interpretative guides for individuals and short, readable books on themes such as career change, workshop support materials, further training options and a constant flow of interesting articles and research. It is unlikely that many other questionnaires will be able to compete here, but this may or may not matter, depending on your purpose and how close a match the rival questionnaire is to the MBTI. If it is a close match, then there is nothing to stop you using MBTI materials alongside whichever questionnaire you have chosen. Look at the resources section on the publisher's website to see what they offer.

Can you take a trial version yourself? When you approach the publishing company, ask if you can try the instrument yourself at no or low cost, with a trained advisor to give you feedback on the results. If this is not possible, ask someone licensed in the instrument to administer the questionnaire and to give you a full feedback session. When you contact the company, note how you are treated: is there a long wait to speak to a knowledgeable person or do they deal with you promptly? Do they treat you courteously and follow up on their promises?

How do you respond to the questionnaire yourself? Pay careful attention to the experience of taking it. Is it easy to navigate the website? Does the questionnaire download easily and with clear instructions? How easy or difficult does it seem to be to answer the questions? Do the items seem well constructed, for instance with unambiguous language? It should not be too easy to guess what they are assessing, so how well does it do this? How many items are there? A large number of items may be off-putting, a small number may convey superficiality. When completing it, does it actually take the time the publishers claim?

Does the resulting report have face validity for you? How well does it describe you, strengths and weaknesses? Subject it to the Barnum test (page 17): could this report describe almost anyone? Is it bland and positive to the point of being meaningless? How is the report presented? For instance, some clients may baulk at a long report, telling you that it contains far too much information or that it is written in language that is too dense for rapid understanding. Some reports have their length bulked out with unnecessary pages for notes on 'action points' which, realistically, few people are ever likely to act upon. A short report may seem vague, skimpy and superficial.

How well does the report read? Watch out for reports which make high-handed statements about an individual who is unknown to the computer generating the report, especially if they annoyingly and perkily address you by your first name throughout. Examples would be, 'Jenny, you are a creative person who does not like detail', a sentence I encountered when I sampled one such questionnaire. No one can reliably make such statements based merely on questionnaire results. The best reports make suggestions and use qualifying words such as 'may', 'could', 'might' or 'sometimes'. There is also an art in how well the software joins different pieces of copy together. In some of the sample questionnaires that I took when researching this chapter, there were places where these joins in the report seemed obtrusive and clumsy with sentences in one part of it that were flatly contradicted by sentences in another and sometimes in the same sentence. An example from one such report was this one: 'Jenny is sensitive, avoids conflict and will pursue the values she believes in to the bitter end, regardless of the impact on other people.' I had to read this sentence several times before dismissing it as the gobbledegook it was.

What other questionnaires or tests does the company offer? Many of the publishers of alternative Jungian questionnaires also offer suites of other questionnaires and tests. Some of these dovetail snugly with their Jungian materials so there could be advantages in using a one-stop-shop approach, for instance if your work involves running development and assessment centres or if you specialize in career coaching.

Some alternative options

I make no attempt here to provide a comprehensive list of the alternative Jungian instruments. I have personally sampled and had feedback on several of them, but this is not the same as undertaking the kind of training which will give you a firm grasp of the aims, benefits and disadvantages of each instrument. For that you will need to investigate on your own terms.

Nor have I listed any of the free questionnaires available on the internet (with the exception of the Keirsey Temperament Sorter below). Most of these free versions are aimed at individuals who are casually browsing. They are intended to be light-hearted, make few claims to validity and are best avoided.

The Keirsey Temperament Sorter (KTS)

Contact: www.keirsey.com

David Keirsey (1921–2013) was a distinguished American psychologist whose work intriguingly combines Jung, Isabel Myers, Gestalt psychology and ancient Greek thinking about personality. When you take his popular Temperament Sorter based on 70 forced-choice questions, one version of which you can do for free on the website and in many languages, you will find that the analysis uses the 16 MBTI labels and that much of it will feel familiar. His book *Please Understand Me* (1998) is widely regarded as an outstanding adjunct and alternative to the classic Type descriptions. However, there are a number of differences between the underlying assumptions in this questionnaire and those of the MBTI. The Keirsey questionnaire is based on observable behaviour rather than on thinking styles. Keirsey's approach groups people into four 'temperaments' (Guardians (SJ), Artisans (SP), Idealists (NF) and Rationals (NT)), unlike the MBTI which groups people by Dominant Function (Thinking, Feeling, Sensing, Intuition). The company offers many other products, most of them reasonably priced, including books, team reports, interest inventories and questionnaires about career and learning styles, some of which are suitable for young people.

What the publishers say

The Keirsey Temperament Sorter®-II (KTS®-II) has been translated into 18 different languages, and has been used by over 40 million people from 140 different countries. It first appeared in *Please Understand Me* (1978), and was updated in the successor *Please Understand Me II* (1998). The KTS-II is currently being used by the Fortune 500, Global 1000, the US Government/Military, by major academic institutions, non-profit organizations, and faith based organizations worldwide.

According to Keirsey Temperament Theory, there are four basic temperament groups which describe human behavior. Keirsey's four temperaments are referred to as Artisans™, Guardians™, Rationals™ and Idealists™. These four temperaments can be further subdivided, often referred to as 'Character Types'. There are four Types of Artisans, four Types of Guardians, four Types of Rationals, and four Types of Idealists.

ARTISAN	GUARDIAN	RATIONAL	IDEALIST
Promoter (ESTP)	Supervisor (ESTJ)	Fieldmarshal (ENTJ)	Teacher (ENFJ)
Crafter (ISTP)	Inspector (ISTJ)	Mastermind (INTJ)	Counselor (INFJ)
Performer (ESFP)	Provider (ESFJ)	Inventor (ENTP)	Champion (ENFP)
Composer (ISFP)	Protector (ISFJ)	Architect (INTP)	Healer (INFP)

Why the Keirsey Temperament Sorter might appeal to you
The Type descriptions are more behaviourally focused than those in the classic MBTI framework. The questionnaires are cheaper to buy and with one version free, though you should note that this gives very limited information. The quirky names given to each Type (see above) are an easy way to remember Type differences.

The Type Mapping System

Contact: Team Focus, www.teamfocus.co.uk

This questionnaire, developed by the British psychologist Roy Childs, is wholly based on Jungian thinking and is designed to appeal to the organizational market. Visually the system is represented as a circle. The developers emphasize Jung's own belief that Type preferences can change over a lifetime. Team Focus offers five variants or 'lenses'. The core questionnaire is called the Type Dynamics Indicator (TDI) with comprehensive information on preferred work environment and style, motivation, possible career choices, strengths and development areas (TDI®-IS). There are 16 possible Types, with the same four-letter labels as in the MBTI, but each Type also has an easily remembered reference, for instance, INTJ is called The Investigator and ISFP is called The Supporter. The company also offers a questionnaire which distinguishes between how you feel you currently are and what you might want (TDI®-WANT). Other options are a Learning Styles questionnaire and two questionnaires based on team working.

What the publishers say
So what we do is to provide three insightful and interlocking perspectives:

- **The inside**, the world of the individual;
- **The outside**, the situation;
- **The in-between**, the dynamics of the relationship.

This is what makes us different and is at the core of what we call Type Mapping.

Type Mapping is an integrated approach based on one comprehensive model, Psychological Type. It brings together individuals (their preferences, identity and aspirations), situations (the context, demands and challenges) and the space in-between (interaction, behaviour and relationships). The mapping can then take place using five 'lenses'; a level of sophistication that allows for enormous flexibility in terms of intervention and development.

Why the Type Mapping System might appeal to you

It is a seriously researched Jungian instrument which avoids the apparent 'boxing' of the classic MBTI but uses the familiar MBTI Type names and offers a number of different lenses with which to view personality. You could support it with all the classic MBTI materials.

Jung Type Indicator (JTI)

Contact: www.psytech.com

The Jung Type Indicator is a wholly Jungian-based alternative to the MBTI. The emphasis is on the organization context. The short questionnaire produces a ten-page report covering areas such as placing you within the familiar 16-cell structure, offering an individualized narrative comment on the eight preferences, working style, management style, thinking style and decision-making. The structure of the questionnaire avoids the dichotomous scoring of the MBTI and acknowledges the on-the-one-hand–on the other-hand behaviour and preferences of people who may score in the middle. Similarly it may offer people two possible 'best-fit' Types. Technical manuals are available free from the website. The company actively seeks licensed distributors and the questionnaire is available in several languages. Psytech offers a whole suite of other assessments such as a trait-based personality assessment using the 16PF and Big Five insights (Fifteen Factor Questionnaire), a general reasoning test and a critical reasoning test battery.

What the publishers say

The Jung Type Indicator (JTI) is a brief, easy to administer, self-report questionnaire that has been designed to help people identify their psychological Type. It has been developed using modern scaling techniques to provide a reliable and valid measure of people's preferences for the psychological functions.

The JTI is an indispensable tool for helping people manage issues of personal change and growth. By providing insight into the fundamental psychological processes, the JTI stimulates self awareness and acts as a constructive framework in which people can understand and explore their interpersonal and thinking styles.

Within organisations the JTI can be used to enhance personal effectiveness and facilitate team building. The JTI questionnaire items are acceptable to people from a broad range of cultural backgrounds, providing a modern, reliable and valid measure of Jungian Type.

Why the Jung Type Indicator might appeal to you

It is faithful to Jung's ideas, quick and easy to complete and allows for 'in the middle' scoring. Although Psytech's support with additional material is limited you could supplement what it offers entirely consistently with materials from classic MBTI sources.

Clarity4D

Contact: Clarity4D, www.clarity4d.com

The Clarity4D model combines Jungian ideas with the ancient Greek notion of the four 'humours': water, fire, earth and air. These are presented as four colours: blue, red, green and yellow. Jungian ideas are reflected in the four-quadrant matrix representing Head v Heart and Introversion v Extraversion. The '4D' stands for four dimensions of personality: how we see ourselves, how others might see us, our hidden potential and the time it takes to develop our potential. The individualized profile is shown on a colour wheel, suggesting how much of each 'colour' the individual person has. The model draws loosely on the idea of preference without using MBTI labels. Each profile will suggest what that individual's strengths might be, how they typically communicate, and how each of their strengths might imply a corresponding weakness (the 'hidden potential').

The developers train and license consultancies and HR professionals ('business partners') to deliver the instrument in countries all over the world. They stress that the instrument is affordable so could be attractive to charities and other non-profit organizations and can be used for young people.

What the publishers say

What does Clarity4D offer me and my clients?

- Simple to understand, no complex graphs for busy clients to absorb
- Affordable to you and your clients, across all levels of organisations and for emerging markets
- Globally understood because of the link to colour and the 4 elements
- Profiles available in Arabic, French, Polish, Portuguese and Spanish
- Effective by incorporating goal setting and action plans into the profile
- No titles or 'putting people into a box'
- Delegates are asked to answer the questionnaire as their instinctive and authentic selves rather than for the role they play at work.

Non-corporate profiles are available for young people and others, enabling closer family communication.

Why Clarity4D might appeal to you

It has readily accessible language and a simple colour system without any of the theoretical complexities of Jungian language. Affordability makes it attractive if your market is individuals or organizations that are cash-poor.

Lumina Spark

Contact: www.luminalearning.com

Lumina Spark is an ambitiously pitched psychometric instrument which aims to combine the insights and approaches of Jungian thinking with the best of the Big Five questionnaires (page 135). It was developed by the British occupational psychologist Stewart Desson. It is a trait-based questionnaire which avoids forced-choice items. Results are presented in a vivid 'splash' of four colours inside a 'mandala' (circle or wheel – in this case an eight-sided figure). The four colours represent 'archetypes', so there is Commanding Red, Conscientious Blue, Empowering Green and Inspiring Yellow. Results will show how much your individual 'splash' involves some of each of these four archetypes. There are no boxes, Types or labels and the questionnaire embraces the complexity of each individual person where it is common to be somewhere in the middle. The individualized report offers three 'personas': an *Underlying Persona*, your natural self; your *Everyday Persona*, the conscious self, you at your best; and the *Overextended Persona*, where you are under stress or overplay your strengths to the point where they become weaknesses.

What the publishers say

Big 5 and 'Best of Jung' – The model is based on the latest Big Five research paradigm, and can also be viewed through the popular Jungian lens.

Trait not Type – Lumina doesn't label people or put them in a box, we call this trait, not Type.

Embraces Paradox – Lumina doesn't force choice of preferences, we call this 'embracing paradox'. We independently measure the level to which each individual has opposite, competing and contradictory aspects of their personality e.g. their level of introversion and extraversion.

Measures 3 Personas – We measure three unique yet integrated views of you – the Underlying you, the Everyday you and the Overextended you.

Simplicity and Depth – We use colourful and practical language to create a set of ideas that people remember and can apply for years to come. The model can be used at a big picture 4 colour level, an 8 aspect level or a detailed full 24 quality level – dependent on your application.

Why Lumina Spark might appeal to you

It combines Big Five thinking with Jungian insights in a single questionnaire. It is trait-based and has a business/organizational slant. Individuals get a comprehensive 40-page report.

Insights® Discovery System

Contact: www.insights.com

Insights began in Scotland with the father-and-son team Andi and Andy Lothian and has now developed into a global business. The questionnaire is available in several languages and countries. It is wholeheartedly based on Jungian thinking. Results are presented on a four-colour wheel which they call 'energies': Fiery Red, Sunshine Yellow, Cool Blue and Earth Green. The wheel then divides into eight 'positions' each of which has a name such as Reformer, Observer, Inspirer. Within this framework the system identifies 72 sub-Types, each with its own highly individualized report. Information is presented in 'chapters'; for example, the Foundation chapter gives an analysis of personal strengths and possible weaknesses, communication style and team contribution. Optional additional chapters offer perspectives on selling style, management style, personal achievement and interview questions to ask job candidates. Like many of the other alternatives to the MBTI, it can be used with teams. The questionnaire sets out to identify shades of preferences in a way that MBTI Step I does not. It differs from the MBTI in how it views Dominant and Auxiliary Functions and instead explores 'conscious' and 'less conscious' personas which, the developers claim, is closer to Jung's original thinking. Like the MBTI, there is an emphasis on strengths and preferences. It is compatible to a moderate extent with MBTI materials and approaches.

What the publishers say

Insights Discovery uses a simple and accessible four colour model to understand an individual's unique preferences. We measure these preferences based on responses to a short online evaluator. One of the outputs is a 20 page personality profile, which identifies strengths and areas for development.

Insights Discovery has its roots in the work of Swiss psychologist Carl Jung. It is continually validated and refined by our research team to ensure it is always accurate and deeply insightful.

Insights Discovery begins by helping you to uncover who you are and how you interact with others. The depth of insight provided means that Discovery can take you to places that you never expected. From one-to-one coaching to team development and improved sales and leadership skills, the possibilities are endless.

Why Insights Discovery might appeal to you

The colour system makes it easily memorable and it can work with groups as well as with individuals. You get an individualized report. It is a neat hybrid of ipsative and normative in its construction.

The Golden Personality Type Profiler

Contact:www.goldenllc.com

This instrument was developed by the American psychologist Dr John P. Golden, a long-time devotee of psychological Type. In structure the resulting report has some resemblances to the MBTI Step II. There is an emphasis on behaviour and on Type development factors; Dr Golden added a fifth dimension, *Tense–Calm*, to measure stress, and the questionnaire embraces both work and leisure environments. The 125-item questionnaire is normative – that is, it avoids forced-choice questions and produces 18 'facet scales' allowing for nuanced interpretations such as being a 'talkative introvert'. One feature of the report is that the familiar J/P scale on the MBTI has been replaced by A/Z, standing for Adapting or organiZing, on the grounds that these words are less misleading than Judging and Perceiving. The Golden questionnaire can be supported by all the classic MBTI materials. It may be especially useful in schools and colleges, and the company provides templates and workshop materials for this purpose.

What the publishers say

Unlike other personality assessments, the Golden Personality Type Profiler is unique in that it:

- Is geared toward identifying behaviors
- Examines both work and leisure situations
- Reports on 36 personality characteristics within the four Global Scales, allowing specific individual personalities to emerge for a more comprehensive understanding of work style
- Has an additional Global Scale not included on other Jungian-based instruments with two additional characteristics measuring responses to daily stressors.

Administered worldwide by schools and organizations in all industry sectors, the Golden Personality Type Profiler is one of the most in-depth personality assessments available. Powered by Jung's Theory of Type as well as the Five Factor model of personality, Golden identifies both a 4-letter Jungian Type and a 5th element for stress while offering 18 sub-facets that describe the unique personality of each individual. Its powerful reporting options for both individuals and teams offer a great insight and better understanding of self and others making Golden the perfect tool for individual and team development interventions.

Why The Golden Type Profiler might appeal to you

It is highly compatible with MBTI materials but avoids the dichotomous structure of the MBTI through giving sub-scales. It might appeal if you were working with young people in schools and colleges or looking for a reasonably priced alternative to the MBTI. The extra dimension which measures stress can be valuable.

Summary

It is worth exploring alternatives to the MBTI as you might well work in organizations which have embraced one of its many rivals. None of these competitors can offer the length and depth of research or the richness of materials associated with the MBTI, but these are not necessarily either/or choices as some of these competitors encourage use of CPP materials as adjuncts to their own. In the end it comes down to your knowledge of your market, what you or your clients can afford and how far any questionnaire meets your particular professional needs. It is unlikely that any one instrument will be an absolutely perfect match to what you need: all have strengths and weaknesses. Most of the rival questionnaires have consciously designed their products to meet common criticisms of the MBTI and you will have to weigh up how important any of these features are against the considerable value of using the original.

4 Doing the debrief: a partnership of equals

You have established that it could be in the client's interests to take the MBTI or one of its Jungian rivals and probably other psychometrics as well. The time to suggest taking it is usually during the first session in a coaching programme, and the most usual place to run the debrief is in the second session.

Fitting the suggestion into the first session

My own practice in a first coaching session with a new client is to undertake a quick review of what I know about why the client feels he or she needs coaching at all. Then I will ask for a brief autobiographical account asking for turning points in their life so far. The first session is also the place for a conversation where the client tells you about family, career, leisure, health and partner relationships. Then we will go on to a more in-depth conversation about goals for the whole coaching programme, including who else might need to be consulted for their input, such as the client's boss. This leads naturally into a conversation about what other development processes they have undertaken.

It is always worth probing what was involved when clients say they have taken a personality Type questionnaire previously. The give-away may be that the client is as vague about when and where this alleged administration took place as they are about what it revealed. 'Oh, I think I was an EPNS', they say, or 'Yes, I'm an ESPN'. (EPNS is actually the acronym for electro-plated nickel silver; ESPN stands for Entertainment & Sports Programming Network – clients who trot one of these out to you may or may not be doing a gently disrespectful leg-pull in order to see how you react.)

Other clients will have encountered the questionnaire on a training course where there was apparently no time for any in-depth explanation. All of this weakens the belief that personality Type has anything much to offer. Some may have benefited from a full debrief in a previous coaching relationship.

It is up to you how you handle this part of the discussion. Possibilities include offering to reinterpret the client's results, suggesting they retake the questionnaire, especially Step II of the MBTI, if the original administration was some time ago; asking the client to let you know what the original results were without offering to reinterpret them; agreeing, if the client feels they have already had more than enough to do with the MBTI, to let the subject drop. Never over-persuade or let yourself look disappointed if the client says no.

When people have not met the MBTI previously, give a brief, enthusiastic but measured description of what it offers and see how the client responds. Because there is more than enough to do in this first session, where clients have expressed an interest in taking it, I usually follow up the session with an email containing reassuring instructions about how to fill the questionnaire in, especially if clients have seemed apprehensive about what the results might reveal.

The debrief at the second session

The debrief or feedback discussion will usually happen in the second session. Take this steadily, allowing a minimum of an hour overall. Where I am debriefing several instruments at once as well as bespoke 360 feedback, I usually plan for a half day.

Stage 1. Mental preparation

I remind myself while I am preparing for the session that everything about the debrief has to mirror the principles of coaching, at the heart of which are choice, equality and respect.

It is absolutely up to the client to decide what relevance, if any, the instrument has for them. Remember that coaching is a partnership and this remains true even when one partner has more specialist information than the other. The coaching client is the world's leading expert on themselves. No matter how much the client discloses to you and how many insights you believe you have into them, you never really know them. Your role is to ask the questions which increase their insight into themselves.

So it doesn't matter what your own apparent insights into the client are; it doesn't matter whether or not the client arrives at some agreed Type profile – it is their privilege to stay confused or undecided if they wish. It is their choice what opinion they have of the MBTI or how sceptical they are about it.

Being willing to abandon pre-conceived ideas about the client
The human brain looks for short cuts. It is easier to work from what we expect or want to be true than to think afresh. None of us is an exception here. There are biological as well as psychological reasons for this. It takes more oxygen and glucose to think through a problem slowly than it does to jump to conclusions. For more on this, read Daniel Kahneman's excellent book *Thinking, Fast and Slow* (2012). Thinking fast – thinking without really thinking – can

lead to *confirmation bias,* looking for evidence to support a pre-existing idea. So if, for instance, you believe all males to be intrinsically less emotionally intelligent than females, you will see apparent facts everywhere to support your view and will miss the plain proof of all the exceptions. It is inevitable that you will have formed some conclusions about the client on the basis of your first session. If you have done the scoring for him or her, then this may have begun shaping your ideas about what to expect in the debrief conversation. However, be prepared to be surprised. Remember that some clients have been masquerading for years as someone they are not and that it is possible, though not at all common, for every one of their reported preferences to turn out to be wrong for them.

Beware, too, of your own 'fast thinking' on Type generally. Avoid using phrases which include words like *always, never, usually* as in 'Sensing people always like tangible evidence'. When describing the preferences, your language should suggest ambiguity, moderation and tentativeness. I like to use phrases such as

> Some people with a Sensing preference can be. . .
> A preference for Judging can sometimes be associated with. . .
> It can be the case that when you have a preference for Intuition you will. . .
> It's possible for people who prefer Feeling to. . .
> This is how this preference is sometimes described and how you reported, but how does that seem to you?

Collect and tell several brief illustrative anecdotes which emphasize the range of possible behaviours associated with each preference, as this will minimize the danger of the client believing that any one story is how people with that preference always behave or that the intention of the MBTI is to box them in.

Stage 2. Contracting and asking about the experience of taking the questionnaire (2–3 minutes)

This sets the tone for what follows. Always do some mini-contracting first. You may have agreed in advance that this session would be spent on the psychometrics, but life events may have intervened and there may be something more urgent that the client would like to discuss: 'We said we would spend this session doing the debrief, but is that still OK by you?'

If you have not already done so, ask the client how much they already know about the MBTI. Ask also: 'What's your own sense of what it would be useful to concentrate on in this session?' Listen carefully to the answer. Even if you did some contracting at your previous session, clients have frequently done their own subsequent investigations through the internet and may already be more informed than you realize. Don't waste their time on information they already have. The same will be true when the client has taken the questionnaire previously, though I find that few can recall much about it. But always check: I remember one client who had sounded vague about what he remembered from a previous administration of the questionnaire but in fact quickly gave elegant and accurate descriptions of the four sets of preferences. I was pleased to have followed my own advice in this case and not to have embarrassed myself by launching into descriptions of what he already knew.

Ask how the client found the experience of taking the questionnaire. Answers may range from enthusiasm because it was intriguing, to indifference or hostility. Whichever it is, ask calmly and warmly for further information:

> So when you say it was 'weird' what was weird exactly?
>
> So you began to guess which questions were about which dimensions – how did that feel?
>
> You say some of the word-pair questions were tricky to answer – can you remember any specific question here?

Where the answer reveals hostility, ask if the client is prepared to go on with the debrief and be absolutely prepared to abort the whole thing if they express anger: 'You seem a bit annoyed and irritated. Do you want to go on?' Just offering to do this is enough usually to reassure the client that they are not going to be forced into taking part in something they disliked so intensely and resistance usually begins to melt away at this point. With other responses, just nod, note them and reassure the client that you will explore and discuss them a little later.

Stage 3. First pass at establishing best-fit Type (10 minutes)

The best kind of debrief on any instrument is *iterative*, that is, you are aiming for ever-deepening understanding by making several rounds of explanation and discussion. This is especially appropriate with the MBTI. In the first pass, my aim is to offer the client several ideas, some of which will be embroidered on later:

> A mini history (a few sentences only) of the instrument, its links with Carl Jung and its distinguished bank of research results
>
> Preference and why it matters, the value of each side of each pair; why the world needs people of each preference
>
> The equality of all 16 Types: no good/bad, better than/worse than
>
> The idea of a best-fit Type along with the uniqueness of each individual.

The concept of preference underpins everything in the MBTI, and I always start with that, using the excellent exercise that I learnt on my training course:

> Write your name (client looks a little startled)
> Now change hands and write your name again
> What was the difference?

The purpose of the exercise is to use handedness as a metaphor – a way of understanding that just as we can use both hands, and can use our non-dominant hand if we have to, using the non-dominant hand will need more deliberate concentration and will virtually always seem more clumsy and childlike. The same is true of preferences. Everyone can and does use all of the preferences every day, but one in each pair will probably be consistently easier and is likely to result in a more skilled performance.

Show the client a simple grid with the four pairs of preferences ('Dichotomies') laid out (Figure 4.1). Explain that the preferences are psychological not logical opposites. Explain that there are common misunderstandings and biases about the desirability of different preferences and that these can be attributed to social norms and unthinking prejudice - for instance, it is worth explaining that Introversion is not the maladaptive response of a shy or neurotic person, it is just one of two equally valid ways of drawing energy (see page 2). Emphasize that the language of psychological Type is different from everyday usage. Make it clear that this is just a first step and that more clarity will probably emerge later.

Stage 4. Comparing the client's first guess with their reported results (45 minutes)

This part of the debrief benefits from being taken slowly. Aim to do more listening than talking. In my role as supervisor of trainee coaches, I have sometimes heard disastrous recordings of this conversation where the coach is so carried away by pleasure in their own expertise and enthusiasm that the client seems to disappear from the dialogue and all you can hear is the occasional faint blur of 'Mmm, I see' in the background. Beware of this danger where the traditional method of explanation can so easily involve the chunk–check–chunk approach, that is, offering the client a chunk of information, pausing briefly to make a cursory check on understanding with a closed question before rushing on to offer another chunk (Figure 4.2). This limits how much the client is able to take in and inhibits exploration, questions, disagreement and disclosure.

Instead, use the pattern of eliciting what the client already knows, listening and summarizing and then in the light of what they have said, offering a brief explanation, then repeating the pattern of eliciting and listening before explaining (Figure 4.3). When you do this you blend what the client raises and knows with what you feel the client needs to know.

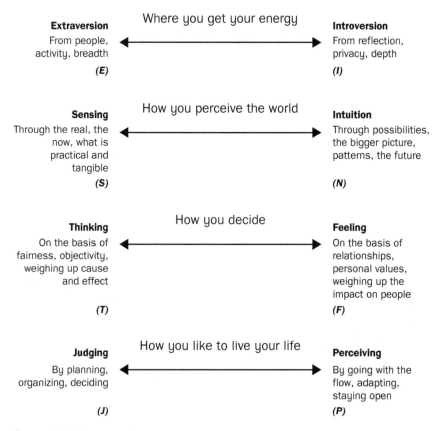

Figure 4.1 The basic preferences

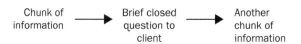

Figure 4.2 The traditional way of giving information

Briefly describe the way the scoring system works – for instance, that although every item is *marked*, this is not true of every *choice*. Explain the concept of clarity of preference where the direction of the score indicates how clear you are that this is what you prefer. Compare the reported score with the client's own earlier guess at where their preference would be on the spectrum. Explain that the questionnaire was always designed by Isabel Myers to be an aid to self-understanding rather than acting as some kind of external examiner on who the client really is.

Talk the client through each of their scores, offering explanations in more detail this time of what each preference actually means, with illustrative

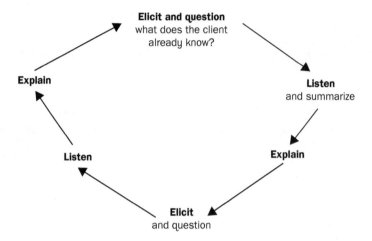

Figure 4.3 Eliciting and listening before explaining

anecdotes. Spend as much time as it needs in discussing what the client's true preference is likely to be without seeming to push the client into coming down on one side or the other if they seem undecided.

Be clear that each preference has potential downsides and describe what these are, asking the client for some examples of their own. Ask the client for his or her own examples of how their preference plays out in daily life. Return to the handedness exercise and ask for examples of how their use of the opposite preference might be more effortful. This is also a good point to introduce the idea that living or working with people of the opposite preference can be challenging: theoretically beneficial to all concerned, but initially often tough because there is so much potential for mutual misunderstanding. Ask for the client's own examples.

Stage 5. Mini-challenges or exercises to clarify each preference (optional, time variable)

Clients are not always immediately clear about their preferences, and why would they be, because they are choosing between two good candidates. You will develop your own favourites but here are some approaches that I find useful:

> *To clarify E/I.* Ask the client what their idea of a perfect weekend away would be, who would be there and what they would ideally do. E-preference people often describe a weekend of jollity with a large party of family and friends, with games, multiple activities and a lot of socializing. I-preference people go for a quiet venue with one or

two close friends with built-in time for one-person activities like reading or solitary walking.

To clarify S/N. Ask the client what they have noticed about the room you are in. S-preference people will often reel off innumerable physical details given as a list. Ns may shrug or look bemused and give you something broad and general. Explain how people of the opposite preference might have responded.

To clarify T/F. This one is harder as many of us, especially women, like to imagine we put relationships first, even if our preference is Thinking. Emphasize that both are equally rational ways of making decisions, and that everyone can call on both and that the Feeling preference is not about 'emotion'. Women may be reluctant to endorse T and men to endorse F, even where it is most probably their true preference. Look out for this when the score is close to the midline. Offer the client a typical T/F dilemma, for instance, having to give an uncomfortable message to someone who is a long-standing friend. While the eventual outcome might be the same, the words used and the tactics described will usually be different. Ts will be briefer and more direct but may emphasize trying to be kind while doing so. Fs will start from the relationship and how to preserve it, often saying they would try more roundabout ways of getting the message across. Ask the client for real performance management examples and how they handled them.

To clarify J/P. Ask the client how they approach a holiday. Do they typically plan a long time in advance? Buy the guidebook? Have each day mapped out? Make lists of things to do before going? Pack the suitcase days in advance? Js may do all of this. Ps will be more inclined to be fans of lastminute.com, flinging a few things into a suitcase the night before and going when and where the whim takes them.

See also Chapter 12 for examples of these and other exercises for use with groups.

Stage 6. Looking at the whole profile (10–15 minutes)

At this point the client may be decisive and clear about all four of their preferences – or they still may not be. Either way, now is the time to hand them a profile and to ask them to read it, taking as long as they like. Where there is doubt about their preferences, suggest they read all of the relevant profiles. Encourage reading in the spirit of scepticism, looking for elements that might be accurate about themselves and elements that are definitely inaccurate. Ask for examples of their behaviour or of feedback they get from others which confirms or challenges each. Many clients are overwhelmed at this point, expressing amazement that *four little letters* could give such a strongly accurate picture of how they see themselves. However, remember the Barnum effect (see Chapter 1) and stress once again that the MBTI has limits, reminding the client of what it was never designed to analyse (adjustment, intelligence, skill and so on). I still remember my own squirm of identification when I read the INTJ profile for the first time and have seen that half-embarrassed, half-amused look of recognition replayed in clients over and over again when they read a profile that fits them well.

Can Type dynamics be useful?

All initial training in the MBTI will tell you that a Jungian Type indicator is more than just letter + letter + letter + letter = who you are. There are many conferences, books and extra training courses that will instruct you in the complexities and mysteries of the theory. Although I rarely explain the actual theory, I do draw on Type dynamics ideas, that is, the possibility that for each Type there is theoretically a hierarchy where the four mental Functions (S, N, T, F) are used in a particular order suggesting a Dominant, Auxiliary, Tertiary and fourth or Inferior Function and will vary according to whether they are used in an Introverted or Extraverted way. The theory says that although these four letters do not appear in the 'letters of Type', we all use all four, and favour some more than others:

> *The Dominant* is the favourite, the one we are likely to trust most
> *The Auxiliary*, taken from the alternative pair of mental Functions preferences, is the supporting act
> *The Tertiary*, the number 3, may not be used so often or so skilfully
> *The fourth Function*, the one Jung thought nearest to the Unconscious, always taken as the opposite of the Dominant, is usually called the Inferior or sometimes the Shadow. This is the one over which we are likely to have least conscious control and which may appear when we are under stress, used in a more primitive and childlike way.

Table 4.1 is a simplified version.

There is controversy about whether research supports these ideas (see page 21). In my own practice, instead of labouring to explain and to persuade the client to accept the complexities of the theory, I use what I find to be useful and instantly understandable ideas through a series of exploratory questions which look at all eight preferences:

> Which of these eight preferences do you feel you can use with ease?
> Which give you most difficulty?
> Of the four 'mental Functions' (S, N, T, F), which do you feel is your favourite – the one you rely on most?

Table 4.1 Simplified list of Type dynamics

Jungian Type	1st (Dominant)	2nd (Auxiliary)	3rd (Tertiary)	4th (Inferior)
ESTJ and ISTP	Thinking	Sensing	Intuition	Feeling
ENFJ and INFP	Feeling	Intuition	Sensing	Thinking
ENFP and INFJ	Intuition	Feeling	Thinking	Sensing
ESTP and ISTJ	Sensing	Thinking	Feeling	Intuition
ENTJ and INTP	Thinking	Intuition	Sensing	Feeling
ESFJ and ISFP	Feeling	Sensing	Intuition	Thinking
ENTP and INTJ	Intuition	Thinking	Feeling	Sensing
ESFP and ISFJ	Sensing	Feeling	Thinking	Intuition

How far is this the one you feel you also use with most skill?

Which is your back-up?

Which of the Functions gives you most difficulty in practice?

Without getting too far into Type dynamics theory, the answers can be enlightening for the client.

Stage 7: The wrap-up (variable time)

In the final stage you might want to link the MBTI results with results on other questionnaires if you are spending an entire session for this purpose. Even where this is not the case, it is worth exploring questions such as:

What are your views now on your Type profile?

What are the implications for you?

What are the implications for the work we will be doing together?

Summary

There is an art in running the debrief where you balance your own knowledge of the questionnaire with the issues that it is vital for the client to explore. Staying open-minded, allowing for the possibility that the client will disagree with their results, and creating plenty of space for discussion will all increase the likely usefulness and enjoyability of the conversation. You may also encounter a number of common challenges from clients, the focus of the next chapter.

5 Common challenges from clients, and how to deal with them

The challenges posed through using the MBTI or other Jungian questionnaires are really no different from any other client-led challenges in coaching. They can all be resolved by remembering that the coaching relationship is in itself challenging as it is unlike virtually any other conversation or relationship the client is likely to have in their everyday lives. However senior, mature, confident and well known the client, behind the public face is a more vulnerable private one that fears exposure and losing control. The client comes for coaching because there is something in their lives that they want to change, yet making such change is elusive. The more important the change, the more elusive it is likely to be and the more resistant the client may prove. The most skilled coach is the one who can work empathetically with the client to understand and dismantle resistance without for a second colluding with them in the pretence that change is not needed. I find it helps to remember some of the most basic precepts of coaching, especially that the client knows him or herself better than you ever can or will and that it is not your job to diagnose, rescue or cure.

What follows are some of the most common MBTI-related challenges with suggested causes, together with some possible ways of dealing with them.

'It's just like a horoscope'

This is a possible response to a first reading of a Type profile and at the stage before you have had the chance to explore the client's preferences in any detail. What is this objection about? The client is sceptical. The client has encountered psychometrics previously and has decided it is all fake science – made up, bland rubbish. The client once heard and now vaguely remembers a critical radio programme or read a magazine article suggesting that psychometrics is a flawed discipline. All of these are possible explanations. The more likely explanation is that the client feels vulnerable, is challenging your expertise and is resisting the idea that the complexities of their personality might be boiled down to a few hundred words of copy – a perfectly legitimate concern.

What to do

Don't ever allow yourself to be provoked into a defensive or prickly response. Smile, nod calmly and acknowledge that this is a familiar immediate reaction, explaining that it is one of the weaknesses of the instrument that arises directly out of one of its strengths, its accessibility. Ask for the client's permission to have the kind of iterative discussion which will show them that the printed profile is the beginning, not the end, of the increased self-awareness which is the whole point of taking the questionnaire in the first place, and that behind the positives which represent mature examples of each Type there lurk some very much less attractive possibilities. You might also like to try this quick corrective to the horoscope accusation. Ask the client to read the profile of their Type opposite to see if they still believe these are like horoscopes:

Rosanna (professor, INTP)

Rosanna was a professor seeking promotion. She had seemed tense and wary at the beginning of our coaching. She had encountered a trait-based psychometric during a previous attempt to change jobs. In a clumsily handled selection process she had had no feedback on the instrument and was inclined to blame it for her failure. 'I'm a scientist', she said. 'I don't believe in horoscopes'. Following the strategy I describe above, I understood that I was not really the target of this possible rudeness, agreeing that a quick first reading could indeed look like a horoscope, but invited her to read the ESFJ profile (her Type opposite). I watched as her eyes widened in disbelief. 'You mean there really are people like this?' she said. That was the last time horoscopes were mentioned.

Don't-knows and midpoint on three or all scores

I have only occasionally met this client, but it is always a possibility to meet them again. The first clue is their response to your question about how it felt taking the questionnaire. They will report finding it 'difficult', saying that their internal question was, 'it all depends'. They may repeat this when you introduce the first stage of the discussion when you describe the preferences and ask them to choose which they feel instinctively is right for them.

There are a number of possible explanations:

The client is genuinely unable to choose between preferences because he or she is equally attracted to all of them

The client is a genius, equally good at all of them

Your explanations of what the preferences mean lack vividness and clarity

There is a low-energy air to the client's interactions with you and it is likely that this is true of how they live their life generally, so there is a can't-be-bothered feel to their choices on preferences

The client is a living example of Imposter Syndrome, telling you that how they are at work (pretence, expecting to be found out at any moment) is radically different from how they are at home

This client never had much interest in coaching or in understanding themselves and couldn't be bothered to fill the questionnaire in, just making random marks or clicks to get the tedious process over with and this is the result

When you had the autobiographical discussion with the client, this revealed chaotic, absent or hostile parenting or a childhood full of shocks, confusions and inconsistencies.

What to do

Explain your dilemma to the client. Say that this is relatively unusual and does not necessarily have a satisfactory ending. Ask how much effort they would like to put into the quest to find a 'best fit' Type. Be guided by their answer. If it is that their level of interest is low, then be prepared to end the discussion quickly. If they want to continue, then try all of the activities and questions suggested in the previous chapter for establishing preferences, plus asking for live examples from the client's life. Explore the Type development area (Chapter 6) and see what happens.

Your coaching will need to take a different direction depending on discussion with the client and whichever of these routes seems the most promising. Of the possible explanations I describe above, the only one I have found to be supported in reality is the last, but I am aware that a very small sample does not constitute evidence:

Delyth (manager, retail banking)

Delyth worked as a middle-senior manager in a retail bank, but things were not going well. She had missed a serious mistake made by one of her team and this had cost the bank a large sum of money. Delyth had been severely reprimanded but had managed to cling on to her job. I offered her the chance to take the MBTI. Extraversion was the sole preference on which she had any clarity and even on that, her preference score was only 7. In our first session I remembered that she had described a sad and challenging childhood. After many years of illness, Delyth's mother had died. Delyth was 10 and the eldest of three children. Lost in his grief, her father had turned to her to be the substitute mother to the other children. No allowance or provision had been made for her own grieving. Delyth had had to learn to cook, clean, do childcare and make the transition to senior school with no time to rebel or be a proper teenager. She had literally had to be all things to all people in her immediate family. She had turned down a place at a leading university to do Sports Science because her father disapproved of a degree that he alleged would lead nowhere and she went instead to a local university for a Business Studies degree and which had allowed her to go on living at home.

Type theory suggests that to be on the midpoint is potentially a source of confusion rather than a sign that you can be equally good at both preferences (though there are versions of Jungian questionnaires where this is possible). I explained this to Delyth, emphasizing that this was just a theory. I asked for her own response. There was a long silence then she said tremulously, 'I have no idea who I really am ...'

The direct link between this and her problems at work was, in her own view, that she had failed to develop a clear understanding of the managerial role and her own style within it, never feeling sure about when to insist and when to give way. Her behaviour was inconsistent; her staff never really knew where they stood with her so never knew when to bring her a problem and when to try to solve it themselves.

Rather than continue the search for preferences in the session itself, I suggested that Delyth's 'homework' was to identify eight moments from personal and professional life where she had felt 'in flow' (see also page 103), to write them down and to bring them along for discussion at our next session, and also to read all eight of the Extravert Type profiles in the hunt for clues to her preferences. This advanced us a little, but only a little, to ES—, leaving four possible profiles. At this stage we agreed that there was little purpose in investing further time in what might still possibly be a pointless quest, so Delyth's 'best-fit' Type remained a mystery. In the rest of our coaching we concentrated on developing a pragmatic set of managerial behaviours which would help prevent a repeat of the dire situation in which she had found herself.

Alternatively, in this kind of scenario you could suggest that the client takes Step II of the MBTI (page 133), which gives nuanced versions of the results and where each of the four dimensions has five sub-facets.

'Not at all like me'

There is a small minority of people whose reported Type when they take the questionnaire is different from how they see themselves. When I get this reaction I remind clients of my belief, to which I alert them before they take it, that it is only a questionnaire, however well constructed, so it can be wrong, perhaps because it is not the very good questionnaire I believe it to be, or because your mood when you filled it in affected your results or because of wanting to fill it in as you would like to be rather than how you really are. A further possible explanation is that the Type profile as written lacks face validity. Remember also one of the core ethical principles of the MBTI, which is that the client is always the best judge of their own preferences.

My own estimate is that around 10% of my clients have doubts about their reported Type, though normally only one preference is disputed. You will be alerted to it in the original part of the debrief discussion where the client's guess is different from what you know of their reported Type. Sometimes the client still doesn't know. If so, that's fine – let it go and maybe make a mental note to return to it later in the coaching, exploring the possibility that the client does not trust their actual preference or is hovering on the midline. Mostly, discussion quickly establishes the client's actual preference and that is the end of the matter.

This issue is only a problem for coaches who believe that the questionnaire has mystical properties and has to be 'right', or who are insecure about their professional expertise and want the pleasure of having chosen an allegedly brilliant questionnaire which the client will accept, thus endorsing the coach's fragile authority. My own view is that in acknowledging that all personality questionnaires have weaknesses you reinforce rather than damage your influence.

Dismay at 'extreme' scores

In running the debrief you will already have explained that according to Type theory, the scores simply represent how clear we are about our preferences, so a score on or near the midline will suggest a very mild preference, or possibly confusion. Similarly, a high preference score means that according to the theory, we are ultra-clear that this is what we prefer. It does not mean, for instance, that we are more or less Introverted or Extraverted or have too much or too little of a preference. This may not reassure some clients:

> I've got a zero for Feeling – does that mean I'm cold?

> Oh dear, my score for Introversion is 45. Am I hopelessly handicapped?

I find myself at odds with the theory here. In practice it may well be that the score is correlated with more or less of the behaviour.

What to do

Explain the theory again. Say that it can sometimes be the case that the direction of the preference scores can indeed represent the way the client behaves. This can be uncomfortable because it may arouse negative feelings associated with unthinking popular stereotypes about the preference, particularly around Introversion/Extraversion and Thinking/Feeling, for instance that an extremely introverted person lacks self-esteem or that a Thinking-preference woman is hard-hearted and ruthless. As with every other aspect of personality Type, the client is the best judge. Ask them what their own belief is. Good questions here are:

> How easy do you find it to access the other half of this Dichotomy?
> What do you feel yourself about whether this represents the amount of the behaviour you actually do that is associated with this preference?

Then, depending on the reply, you can initiate a Type-development discussion (see Chapter 6) where you explore the possible consequences of over-relying on one preference.

'I looked all this up on the internet'

Between the session where you have suggested taking the MBTI and the one where you do the debrief, the client has energetically researched the topic, sometimes including retaking the questionnaire through one of the free or cheap internet versions. Sometimes such research has focused on criticisms of the instrument – which are not hard to find. Some, especially INTPs and INTJs, come to the debrief session armed with sheaves of printouts. I was supervisor to a coach who ruefully reported falling into the trap of squabbling with the client over the allegedly poor quality of the client's research, foolishly but understandably asserting the superiority of her own training – and losing the client. It is a mistake to see such client-initiated research as aggressive, though it may present like this. The client has been interested enough to do some homework. Bear in mind that just as at least 25% of medical information on the internet is plain wrong, the same is likely to be true of the random searches on the MBTI done by your client. Also remember that the MBTI has some well-known imperfections and that the client may have identified them.

What to do

- Suggest the client talks you through what they have found out
- Ask how they respond to this and summarize their reply
- Give the client's research a quick read and note its source. Be prepared to learn something new and interesting
- Ask permission to give your own perspective, avoiding getting unhelpfully defensive, but also being prepared to answer weak criticisms with appropriate evidence, respectfully offered
- Where the client has academic interests, or seems likely to want to pursue it further, refer them to the CAPT site (www.capt.org) and stress the comprehensive nature of the research they will find on this site, saying that you will be interested to know what they discover.

Once you have the client's permission to explore their findings, pause the debrief to ask how this fits with the client's own research. Often it does – a bit:

Katherine (management consultant, INTP)

This was a young client of fearsome intelligence, as she constantly reminded me – a starred first-class degree in Philosophy at Cambridge and now working in a high-prestige consultancy – but not tremendously happy, as it turned out. Katherine's instinct was to wrestle me on intellectual authority, a challenge I politely declined, explaining that my role was not to be one of her dons at Cambridge. If we were to work together then the emotional arena, Feeling (bear in mind that if Type dynamics theory is correct this would be the Inferior Function for an INTP), was important. Underneath her braggadocio Katherine was formidably insecure, given to apparently uncontrollable tantrums about which she was ashamed and worried. She came to her second session announcing that she had 'found out all there was to know about INTP, and all of it suggested INTPs were the worst possible Type to be'.

'Tell me what you've researched that says this?'

'Well, all of it really.'

'Specifically ...?'

There was no 'specifically', just a jumble of randomly assembled 'facts' from dubious websites.

Quietly I talked her through the classic INTP profile, asking for her comments. In fact, INTP was in theory a good fit for her then current job, and our coaching concentrated on how to get leverage from the upsides and to minimize the downsides. But this job turned out not to be such a good match for Katherine's many skills, and within a year she had found a much more comfortable fit, a fellowship at a university.

'Don't want to be this Type'

Here the client agrees that their preferences are the ones reported through the questionnaire. But they don't like what they read. The probable explanations are:

- It is a reminder of early-life disapproval from parents
- There is some mentor figure in their lives who represents a different Type
- They are at odds with the dominant preferences in their organization
- They are over-affected by the negative aspects of some or all of the preferences
- It is not actually their 'best-fit' Type.

Handle this calmly. Ask:

What is it you don't like, specifically?
What does this suggest in relation to your autobiographical account?

Alternatively, offer the client an alternative version of the same Type profile to read, or explore which Type might be a better fit.

I like Isabel Myers' phrase about being 'psychologically patriotic', in other words, be pleased and proud to be your Type, accept its weaknesses and exploit its strengths, and I often quote this to clients. Rather than seeing this declaration from a client as a crisis, I see it as a wonderful opportunity to explore identity, career, relationships – and everything else that coaching can involve. This kind of response to the MBTI often comes from the client who tells you that they lack confidence. They will report finding it hard to speak up at meetings or to disagree with colleagues. Frequently they will have problems with delegating – and its close companion, working excessively long hours. You will need to tackle all of this through your normal coaching approaches, but in terms of the MBTI you may find that the client does indeed seem to be unable to access the positive behaviours associated with their Type:

Gideon (family doctor, ISFJ)

Gideon was working in a large inner-city medical practice. The presenting issue was career: Gideon reported wanting to leave medicine, a massive and potentially no-turning-back decision, because he found it 'boring and unfulfilling', yet said he felt compelled to stay because of the huge investment that had been made in his education and training. He said that he felt 'oppressed' by his colleagues and claimed that he got 'landed with all the rubbish jobs and patients'.

Debriefing the MBTI was a revelation to him. 'Yes, this is me', he said, 'but I wish it wasn't'. Gideon only saw the downsides of ISFJ: deep Introversion, a narrow focus on facts, pessimism about the future, fear of making a mistake in diagnosis, a horror of disagreeing and a tendency to be too passive along with occasionally fighting back with spite or half-hidden aggression.

I promised that we would look at career options, but suggested that first we should explore what the positives of ISFJ would mean for his practice as a doctor, saying that I felt that whatever career he followed, his ISFJ profile would go with him. We spent 90 minutes on this discussion. Gideon left with a notebook full of new behaviours to try – all on a strictly limited trial basis.

Gideon stayed in medicine. I think of him as a rare example of an MBTI session being the clear turning point in a coaching programme. It gave him permission to be the best possible version of himself, though as he commented in our wrap-up conversation after 12 hours of coaching, 'I do realize this is a lifelong process.'

'This Type doesn't seem to be a good fit with my profession, does it?'

This question may be put in a number of different ways, for instance by a client who asks you straight out which jobs are likely to suit their Type preferences. Career-focused coaching is never about gazing into your special Type-secrets crystal ball and pronouncing confidently, 'Oh yes, I think you should be a lawyer.' It is true that there are many research projects which have shown correlations between Type preferences and particular professions, but this is not the same as saying that the only people who can do that work successfully are people of that Type. When clients come for career-focused coaching I clarify at the outset that it is not my role to fit a client to a job: I do not have the knowledge this would need (and doubt whether anyone could, given the explosion of jobs that has happened in the last 40 years), and there is a mass of information out there which the client can search for him or herself without needing my help. Type is just one part of career choice: competence, maturity, enthusiasm, age, education, qualifications and life circumstances are all equally important.

Possibly far more important is to challenge yourself about any preconceptions you might have about which Types may be successful and happy in any given role. For instance, Intuitive-preference Types and Feeling-preference Types seem to be underrepresented in surgical roles, but this does not mean that, say, an ENFP could not make a fulfilling career as a surgeon. It would be unethical for you to discourage such a client on the grounds that an ENFP surgeon is allegedly a rarity. Instead, use questioning to explore how they view the role and what they feel their preferences would contribute to it. I do find it to be true that such questioning may well reveal a poor fit between the client's current career path and their Type preferences (I have given some examples in this book) but it would be rash to assume that this is always the case. In an earlier career I appointed an excellent business manager whose preferences were ENFP. Her role was one that you would expect to see fulfilled by an ESTJ, but in fact she was highly numerate and saw her job as a way of using her skill with numbers and processes to help our business clients to get the outcomes that they wanted.

'Can I be a leader if I'm not one of those TJ Types in the corners?'

This question is really just another version of the previous question. My own book of profiles has a histogram which shows the distribution of results from a large and constantly updated sample of managers. Like many similar pieces of research it demonstrates that the Thinking–Judging Types can dominate in leadership roles, along with ENTP and ESTP. This can be initially dismaying to the many senior manager clients whose profiles are different.

In the discussion that follows, I cover the following points:

> The fact that so many organizations choose people of these Types does not mean that they are wise choices, only that organizations are attracted to the behaviours which those Types can represent
>
> Once this becomes the dominant set of profiles, selectors tend to look for people just like themselves
>
> Too many similar Types, especially TJ Types, in a leadership cohort leads to familiar weaknesses: over-rating firmness, forgetting the importance of flexibility and the people dimension – flaws that are often directly associated with organization failure
>
> It is possible to be a successful leader with any of the 16 Type profiles, though the leadership styles will be radically different (and I give some examples, carefully anonymized)
>
> When you are different, you may need to understand in detail – and then respect – how you add value to the organization.

When you are conspicuously different it is important to be able to learn how to negotiate and work with the many people whose Type preferences are not the same as yours:

Thom (student leader, ENFP)

My typical client is a senior leader in a large organization, but Thom was different. His dad, a former client, referred him to me. Thom, an aspiring politician aged 27, was about to become a PhD in Psychology and was a student leader. His MBTI profile was unequivocally ENFP. Immediately he was intrigued by the difference between his preferences and those of the traditional Thinking-preference leader, not least his preferences for F and P. I told him that my guess was that several former US presidents, living and dead, had F and P preferences (for example, Bill Clinton, Ronald Reagan, Gerald Ford, Jimmy Carter). Our coaching was immediately directed to how an ENFP could get leverage from this style rather than trying to beat all those NTs or STs at their own game and then on to learning how to understand their typical ways of thinking and behaving in order to influence them effectively.

Summary

Clients will present familiar challenges and questions on taking a Jungian questionnaire. The solutions are always about treating their questions respectfully and being aware of any tendency of your own to over-invest in how 'correct' any one questionnaire can be.

6 Developing and growing

All coaching is about developing and growing, though bear in mind that no client ever comes to coaching asking for 'personal growth' or to 'tap into their inner resourcefulness', both of these being phrases that unfortunately are all too common on coaches' websites. This chapter explores how Jungian ideas about 'Type development' can be useful in coaching. It also looks at the topic of why Type can help in managing stress.

There is a difference in any coaching session between one where the client's aims are purely transactional and one where the aims are transformational. Transactional issues are one-offs about solving a particular problem such as how to manage a specific poor performer. Transformational issues are about learning a whole new approach which you can apply to any similar situation and will be as much about the client as about the other person. All coaches work on transactional problems – it is part of what we do every day – but coaching is at its most satisfying for coach and client when it is transformational and therefore involves development and growth.

Jung's idea was that our preferences are inborn and that we are engaged in a lifelong journey towards what he called *individuation*, meaning developing into the best possible version of ourselves. I like this idea: it is close to everything that has driven me throughout my career, whether it was when I was teaching the gifted, non-English-speaking, 16-year-old children of recent immigrants (my first job), or making educational TV programmes (mid-career) or working with senior executives and other coaches (as I do now). Little frustrated me more as a young teacher than seeing unfulfilled potential in my students, and I feel the same now about my senior clients. The idea of individuation, closely associated with *differentiation*, is the opposite of all that simplistic thinking which assumes that Jungian profiles stereotype people.

Type development

The idea of *Type development* is embedded in the MBTI. Type development assumes that conscious and unconscious processes are at work throughout our lives: in early life we ideally develop and trust our Dominant Function, growing all its associated skills; in mid-life we might achieve the balance of a healthy Auxiliary Function; and in later life may experiment with the Tertiary or even with the Inferior or fourth Function. (See also page 56). The essential Type preferences may remain the same but how we use them may and ideally should develop. This is not about becoming equally effective in all eight preferences. It is about greater awareness, balance and maturity.

'Good Type development' is about healthy pride in our preferences, awareness of our associated blindspots, humility about understanding and drawing on the opposite preference when we need to, often in support of our Dominant and Auxiliary Functions. Doing this means we are more likely to be consistent, stable and mentally healthy people. In this way personality Type concepts are radically different from trait theories where the assumption is that it is better to be a little bit of everything.

What gets in the way?

There is no doubt that social pressure is a mighty force for distorting trust and confidence in our innate preferences. Extraversion is valued more than Introversion in many societies, including our own. You can see this in everyday school gate conversations where parents worry about a child who seems quiet and more content with their own company than with constant socializing. This can be a real worry – the child lacks the confidence to mix – or a baseless worry – the child can socialize perfectly well when he or she wants to and also needs time alone. I have heard many versions of the story where a parent whose own preference was clearly Extraversion was worried about a child who liked solitary activities: 'You've always got your head in a computer/book. Why aren't you out playing with other kids?'

Judging often seems to be rated more highly than Perceiving, since Judging is associated with conscientiousness and planning. These vague impressions of what is valued and what is not can sometimes distort behaviour when the person's own preference is different.

Gender stereotypes

Gender, too, plays an influential role in development. Girls grow up in most societies believing that their role is to nurture. Boys are told not to cry. These gender stereotypes are constantly reinforced, despite so many years of feminism and formal legislation around equal opportunities. Such pressures may mean that a Thinking-preference woman may struggle with the idea that her natural preference is for logic and rationality, while a Feeling-preference man may dread being labelled as 'soft'. You will see every kind of adaptive or maladaptive behaviour in the coaching room as a result:

Marni, ESTP, dressed in overtly masculine clothing despite being entirely heterosexual, on the basis of the attitude, 'see if I care if you think I'm tough and mannish!' During our coaching she came to see that others regarded this as provocative and childish and that it was entirely acceptable for a woman to have a preference for Thinking.

Tracey, ISTJ, dreaded being thought 'tough' or 'butch' and had cultivated a high, girlish voice along with a clothing style which included pastel colours plus many ruffles and flounces. Anger was a perpetual issue for her and she was being treated for depression. Learning that a preference for Thinking was completely compatible with femininity was liberating. I referred her to a speech therapist who quickly worked with her to develop her natural voice. A more streamlined clothing style gradually emerged along with the deeper voice and, whether by coincidence or not, the depression melted away.

Joseph, ENFP, had learnt as a child that expressing emotions such as gentleness and kindness drew ridicule and isolation in his rural family and school. As an adult, he had serious difficulties at home because he was totally unable to express his grief after the unexpected death of a young son. His wife had denounced him as 'cold and uncaring'. Joseph told me that he had had so little practice in talking about his feelings that he felt literally tongue tied and had no vocabulary to describe them, though he longed to do so. Much of our coaching centred around exploring what a feelings vocabulary would consist of and practising using it.

Giovanni, ESFP, already feeling like an outsider because he was the only gay man in his team, and not 'out', said that at work he did what he called 'miming masculinity and not doing it very well'. It was a relief to him to discover that having a Feeling preference did not mean that he was 'irrational' and that being gay had nothing to do with the Feeling preference.

Organization culture

Many years ago I worked in Chicago as one of the faculty on a project for the now long-defunct accountancy firm Arthur Andersen. In an extensive consultancy and coaching career I cannot think of any assignment that I have disliked more. The participants, all senior partners, had been told that it was compulsory to take the leadership course we were running, so they were already sulky and rebellious. Worse, they saw it as an irritating distraction from their main aim in life, which seemed to be about making a lot of money, even though many had proudly described themselves in the opening ice-breaker as 'independently wealthy'.

The course was meant to support a new, broader and more relationship-based consultancy role for the company. On the second day of a five-day event, we administered, explained and coached them in the MBTI. There were 40 participants. Thirty-eight (95%) had preferences for ISTJ, and I believe this result was broadly repeated in the later courses (in which I did not take part). It fell to me by chance to coach one of the two people (and one of only four women) in the group, who were the exception to the ISTJ rule. In the privacy of the coaching room she briefly broke down as she described her horror at having been 'outed' as an ENFP in front of her colleagues, in other words, been exposed as different. She described her intense dislike of the Andersen culture where she said conformity was rigorously imposed not just in the gloomy formal clothing all employees were enjoined to wear, but also in attitudes and work practices which she claimed included unethical behaviour towards clients. What kept her there? She was the breadwinner in her marriage, had a severely disabled husband dependent on her medical insurance and believed she was caught in the money trap just as much as her colleagues. She was already fully aware of her difference from her colleagues, not just in gender but also because of her difficulty in conforming to the behaviour she saw all around her. Learning about Type gave her a new way of thinking about this. 'I try my best to be a good little ISTJ,' she said, 'but it's so exhausting!'

My guess is that if Andersen had recruited others at the graduate stage who were different from the prevailing ISTJ profile, most would have found some reason to leave quickly or would have been forced out. The event itself was a challenging exercise in Type differences as without exception all eight of us in the faculty had preferences for NT, so no wonder we – and our participants – found it hard going. What the firm wanted was more NT and NF behaviour, but this powerful group of ISTJ professionals could not for the life of them see what was wrong with how things were.

It was no surprise to me some years later to learn of Arthur Andersen's role as neglectful auditors in the deplorable conduct of the US energy company, Enron, whose spectacularly criminal behaviour resulted in several of their most senior executives going to prison. Andersen collapsed in Enron's wake, and maybe it is not too fanciful to wonder if this might have been averted had they been able to create a different culture with a more diverse range of Types.

Organizational culture can easily create, sustain and reinforce a psychologically narrow view of the world. My anecdotal evidence about Arthur Andersen is an extreme example, but I have seen many others. It can happen so easily. First, you would naturally recruit the people who seem to have the skills needed to deliver the essential products or services you were offering. The chances are that these would be associated with particular Types. So an accountancy practice would indeed be likely to attract and need STJs. The company is successful and the initial recruits become more senior. They will probably recruit others in their own image. Soon the culture becomes hostile to people who don't fit, so such people either are never selected and promoted or else they leave in short order.

At the BBC where I worked for many years as a staff member and later as a consultant and coach, it is clear that the organization chooses and promotes NTs for its production departments. This is not a surprise as the skills needed for broadcast production are exactly the ones you would expect NTs to have. The question is not whether this is 'wrong', as I believe it is inevitable, but how aware people are of the consequences, especially for those who seem different.

What happens when you don't 'develop' your Type?

One of the main ways in which Type can be useful in coaching is in spotting how life events have prevented the client from developing their true Type preference. The results can be anything on a spectrum of vague awareness of not reaching potential to a catastrophic sense of failure. Look out for these symptoms:

Lack of trust in the Dominant Function and timidity about using it. The following case study is typical:

Eleanor (production control executive, ISFP)

Eleanor grew up in a military family with parents who valued what they called 'straight talking' and academic achievement. She did well at school and won a place at a good university. From there she joined a graduate scheme with a car manufacturer and excelled on the technical side, learning how to run a factory and, much later, to manage a key part of the organization's business. When she came for coaching it was because she felt 'adrift', cut off from her peers and from the large team she managed. Eleanor's reputation was for fierce, demanding and prickly behaviour with a focus on efficiency. I expected that she would report as ESTJ. Instead her preferences were ISFP. 'This is who I really am', she said. In discussion she broke down as she described a lifelong impression that what she came to understand as the Feeling preference was not OK; she had held back from having children for this reason. She said that her 'real' life was at home with her loving husband, her cats and her beautiful garden. No one at work had any idea about any of this. Masquerading as an ESTJ, she had never developed her Dominant Feeling preference and said she was 'queasy' about trusting it, nor was she using any of the ESTJ preferences skilfully. The focus of our coaching then became what it would mean in practice to do this and the impact it might have on her leadership style if she did. At a team day, Eleanor shared her results along with everyone else, to general astonishment, and this in itself was the beginning of a major shift in her leadership style and one much more suited to the team she led.

Never developing a balancing Auxiliary. An INTJ (Dominant Function N) may have neglected their Auxiliary T, and thus be forever in the grip of new ideas and grand plans for the future without ever subjecting any of them to rational analysis. An ESTJ (Dominant Function T) may ignore the data which suggests that their ideas are not supported by the evidence, rushing to judgement far too soon.

Lack of self-awareness. An Extravert who has no ability to draw on Introversion may not realize how much they over-talk and how noisy and brash they seem to others, including to other Extraverts. An I who never learns some E skills is forever at risk of seeing others as the source of their problems with the external world and retreating even further into themselves, thus further cutting off useful challenges.

Looking and feeling inauthentic through trying to be something that the client is not. Clients may report that they feel like impostors or are exhausted by the effort of always having to turn in a performance, as in this example:

Andrew (insurance company executive, INTP)

Andrew had been referred to me by his boss as a last chance before asking him to leave. Privately she told me she wondered if he had a hearing problem because he spoke so loudly and often did not seem to hear what was said to him. In talking Andrew through his autobiography in our first session, he told me that he had been viciously bullied at his boys' school for being 'quiet'. For 'quiet' read 'introverted'. At 15 he had decided that he therefore needed to be loud, sporty, noisy, jolly and constantly talking: in effect, an ESTJ. This of course was an act. He won a scholarship to Oxford. The strain of pretending to be so different from his true self was such that he told me he retreated every evening to a secret spot on the roof of his college, whatever the weather, as it was the only place where he could get 'peace'. He had never heard of the concepts of Introversion and Extraversion as used in the MBTI. I encouraged him to be totally candid when filling in the questionnaire and to answer according to what he really felt. I have literally never seen such relief on a client's face as on Andrew's when I debriefed his questionnaire where his score for Introversion was 49 and for Extraversion 3. There was no problem with his hearing, but his lack of authenticity was obvious to close colleagues. They spotted and were puzzled by his odd behaviour.

Andrew is an extreme example of social pressure to be more extraverted than you really are. In his case it had resulted in a failure to develop the skills of Introversion at the same time as being an unconvincing Extravert, along with undeveloped Intuition. It also meant that he expended palpable quantities of negative energy in trying to be something he was not. He was able to reassess his job and recalibrate it in a way that kept both him and his boss happy. Today I would make sure he had the chance to read Susan Cain's book, *Quiet* (2013), about the joys and advantages of Introversion as a balance to the dominance of belief that somehow extraverted behaviour should be the norm.

Trying to be all things to all people. The client will seem inconsistent; people will never be quite sure who they are dealing with.

Over-relying on one preference. Clients may dismiss the opposite preference – for instance, a T may declare that feelings are 'ridiculous' or 'sentimental', confusing the Feeling preference with mawkishness. A P who can never access J and tells you that J is just about over-caution, may become a charming ditherer, forever changing their mind, unreliable and unable to plan. An N may mock Sensing as 'fixated on micro detail' and be unwilling to see how sloppy he or she can become as a result. Such views will not only limit the client's actual performance but also suggest that he or she strikes colleagues as rigid and prejudiced. Such clients may overuse the strengths of a preference to the point where such strengths become weaknesses. Sometimes even the most senior people can become stuck when this happens, in this case over-using a Dominant Feeling preference:

Brennan (creative director, advertising agency, ENFJ)

The world of advertising and media needs and encourages innovation. Empathy is valued. Brennan had been successful in his career without realizing that he had often been promoted as a way of avoiding challenging him and of getting around the chaos that he unintentionally created. Brennan made close and positive relationships with the agency's clients. He understood the core of their brands, he 'got it' in terms of how their values also created brand value. Brennan was warm and empathetic; he talked about his 'boys and girls' without noticing the wincing that this created in a team which increasingly included 'Millennials' and who found these labels outdated and offensive. He ran awaydays where the purpose seemed to be to get everyone to agree with him, with, as one of his direct reports said, 'old-fashioned campfire folksiness'. When people brought him data which challenged his belief that the future for the business was rosy, he rejected it, saying that he 'couldn't bear negativity'. Colleagues learnt to manipulate his overwhelming need to be liked. This meant that people quickly found that no decision was ever final because it depended on who had last talked to him. Brennan came for coaching when his company was taken over by a tougher and more successful rival and the new managing director saw immediately that Brennan's way of leading was a business risk. In our coaching, Brennan had to learn first that his unrealistic optimism and unwavering dependence on heart over head was disastrous and that his refusal to use Thinker logic was potentially a career crash in waiting.

I like the idea that in later life we can consciously develop even our Inferior Functions. This was exactly what this client discussed with me:

Jolande (INTJ, headteacher, planning retirement)

Jolande was so good at her job that she had often been drafted in to help 'failing' schools. A wonderful example of a well-rounded INTJ, she was patient, insightful, inspirational in her own teaching and with her staff, constantly attracted to new ideas in teaching and learning – a natural leader. She had learnt to pace her innovations by working well with people whose Dominant Function was Sensing where their practicality could balance her vision. As she headed towards retirement from teaching she had many offers of consultancy work, but in her coaching with me, she became fascinated by the idea of 'good Type development' and commented that she was already experimenting with her two least preferred Functions: Feeling and Sensing. The Feeling preference she planned to develop even further by taking on childcare for her young grandchildren two days a week and the rest of her time she planned to devote to gardening, walking and learning flamenco dance, these last three being entirely Sensing activities. 'I need grounding' she said, 'I've spent so much of my life on intangibles. I know I'll never master flamenco, but nothing is going to stop me trying!'

Stressed clients

We tend to bandy around the word 'stress' to the point that it is talked about in organizations as if it is an actual illness, which it is not. 'She went off with stress' is a common way to talk about people who have taken time off because they simply cannot bear whatever burdens their work or lives are creating, with resulting physical or mental health problems. There is a difference between pressure and stress. Pressure can be enjoyable; if there is no pressure, work can become dull. But too much pressure can quickly develop into overwhelming demands that feel intolerable. The more senior the job, the more likely it is that long hours become the norm, with many high-level, knotty problems where there is no obvious solution. The fantasy that if only we can work harder and longer we can somehow solve these problems can become all-pervading, driving yet more commitment to work with fewer and fewer tangible results and more and more serious damage to physical and mental health.

Whatever our Type preferences, our responses to stress are essentially the same. First we step up whatever tactics normally work: trying harder to be even more efficient or competent or likeable or ingenious, depending on our Type preferences. Under extreme stress this probably doesn't work at all, so we panic. Then we lose perspective: it is impossible to stand back, or even to ask yourself what this problem would look like in a week's time, let alone a year ahead. We become humourless, we can't be teased or jolted out of our misery with a joke. Thinking narrows to off–on choices; it becomes digital, there is only black or white, right or wrong, as shades of grey disappear; we feel out of control.

You will have your own successful suite of approaches for working with clients to defuse their stress. In my own work I find that the common themes involve learning how to delegate, something a surprisingly large number of bosses have never managed to do; learning how to interrogate their own thought processes so that they gain some perspective; understanding the neuroscience and biology behind the experience of stress and knowing how to play the brain at its own game with techniques such as controlled breathing, mindfulness and meditation.

Where Type concepts can help is in understanding what the likely patterns of stress are for any one Type. The theory is that when you take the four mental Functions (Sensing, Intuition, Thinking, Feeling) the 'Inferior' Function is the one most likely to erupt during times of stress (see also page 56). The theory suggests that when under stress there will be a two-stage process. First we will try redoubling our reliance on what usually works so well for us: our Dominant Function. If the stress edges upwards, we can flip into using our Inferior Function, and because it is rightly labelled the Inferior by being nearest to the Unconscious, we will use it in a childlike, uncontrolled way. These phenomena have often been explored in fiction, most famously in Robert Louis Stevenson's novella, *The Strange Case of Dr Jekyll and Mr Hyde*, first published in 1886.

Being 'in the grip'

The phenomenon of being out of control when experiencing an upsurge from your Inferior Function is known in MBTI theory as 'being in the grip'. In terms of current understanding of neuropsychology, it means that the limbic system of the human brain, its emotional centre, has taken over from the prefrontal cortex, its rational areas. It means that we behave in ways that seem completely alien, we don't recognize ourselves:

> I obsessed about silly details, I lost things, I turned into a hypochondriac, I shouted a lot. Where had that calm competent person gone? (INTJ)

> Rationality is my middle name, but during the time of that period at work when I was held responsible for an IT system that had comprehensively failed, I was basically crazy – I believed everyone was my enemy. It seems incredible now. I just lost my focus and all my perspective; I felt like a 5-year-old. (INTP)

> I just went away and basically hid for three days after I was told that I was going to be made redundant. Thirty-five years of experience and phtt! Go away!! I really did feel 'beside myself'. It wasn't me. I couldn't talk. And then I went on a very long bender for the first and only time in my life. (ESTJ)

My husband had left, the marriage was over. I thought, OK, no marriage, no social status, alone, old, neglected, complete failure, I've got no future and everything everywhere is getting worse and worse anyway, climate change, horrible politicians. Fortunately I had two good friends who refused to let me be alone and just listened, but that bleak utterly fantastically illogical way of thinking was overwhelming. (ESFJ)

I had an upsetting appraisal conversation with my boss. I felt I had been stabbed, there was no other word for it, it was so unfair; I'd thought we were friends, not just colleagues. After crying a lot I fantasized about violent revenge – yes really, this nice, jolly person, i.e. me, was contemplating how great it would be to murder him. It wasn't pretty. (ENFP)

Most Type profiles will give information and hints on this. One way to think about it is to read the profile of your Type opposite but to imagine that you have all its downsides and are using everything it describes but in the most unsophisticated possible way.

Another simple way to remind yourself of how it works is to consider how stress affects the different temperaments (see Table 6.1).

There is practical value in this approach to stress. It offers clients an explanation for what otherwise seems inexplicable and upsetting. It normalizes people's reactions and by doing so helps them to recover. In the longer term there is also much to be learned from these eruptions from our Inferior Function: they are part of who we are. If you are interested in drawing on this material, show it to the client, discuss whether they recognize the typical triggers and responses. This brings more conscious awareness.

To help them avoid or to manage similar episodes in future you might explore:

How could you recognize the early signs that an 'in the grip' episode could happen?

What has worked in the past as a way of avoiding or shortening its length or moderating its intensity? Most people will mention consciously altering their physical state by going for a walk, meditating, doing some mindfulness exercises or making themselves seek out a friend who can be relied upon to listen carefully and without offering platitudinous advice.

What resources – people, specific strategies and so on – will help another time?

You might also want to consult two helpful books here: *Was That Really Me?* by Naomi Quenk (2002) is a detailed exploration of how the Inferior Function works, with portraits of how it may affect particular Types. Carole Pemberton's book *Resilience: A Practical Guide for Coaches* (2015) describes innumerable

Table 6.1 How stress affects different types

TYPE	TRIGGERS	MANIFESTS FIRST AS...	THEN AS...
SJ	Controls breaking down	Redoubled efforts to control	Seeing only doom and gloom ahead; ignoring the facts
	Too much change too quickly	Unable to delegate	Obsessive planning for apocalyptic scenarios
	Traditional values breached	Coming down hard on those around them	
	Systems not working properly	Angry, irritable	Catastrophizing
	High levels of ambiguity; not knowing what is happening	Getting insensitive and insistent; ignoring people's feelings	Giving way to crying or other emotional outbursts and can't stop
	Airy-fairy talk about 'vision'	Seeming not to notice that important relationships are in danger	Taking risks, behaving rashly and impulsively
	Denied a part in planning for the future	Stubbornness	
SP	Heavy-handed control with personal autonomy severely limited	Becoming an observer, being passive-aggressive	Running away
	Too much seriousness; lack of fun	Making inappropriate jokes	Getting transfixed by religion, political extremes, mystical experiences
	Too much theory and abstraction	Creating a crisis to see what will happen	Letting a powerful figure dominate you
	Rigid objectives and emphasis on planning	Staging ill-judged pranks	Getting involved in risky relationships
	Perpetual monotony, predictability and routine	Challenging superiors unwisely	Breaking down

(Continued)

Table 6.1 (continued)

TYPE	TRIGGERS	MANIFESTS FIRST AS...	THEN AS...
NF	Complex moral dilemmas	Getting too involved in other people's problems	Bitterness
	High levels of conflict at work or at home	Making pointless sacrifices	Taking every criticism, even the smallest, personally
	The loss of a friendship	Taking all the blame	Claiming to be isolated and loveless
	Observing cruelty or other kinds of distress where it is not possible to intervene	Working too hard on hopeless causes	Becoming hysterical
	Being criticized, especially for a breach of an important personal value	Saying yes when you mean no	Lashing out with blame even against those who are blameless
	Working with unhappy people	Overworking	Spite: trying to hurt those who love you most
	Feeling at odds with the values of those around you	Getting moralistic and emotional	Becoming apathetic
NT	Not having the skill or competence needed for the task	Becoming super-rational	Obsessing about small physical details
	Dealing with bureaucracy	Dreaming up even grander plans and visions	Losing important personal possessions – keys, money, passport
	Mind-numbing routine and detail	Getting petty and pedantic	Getting in a muddle about dates and times
	Being accused of incompetence by someone you respect	Criticizing others harshly over small failures	Missing deadlines
	Dealing with incompetent people	Overworking specifically in order to prove others wrong	Making beginner mistakes
	No opportunity for creativity	Becoming ultra-competitive over even the smallest issue	Eating and drinking too much
	Insistence on hierarchy		Childish rebellion; 'working to rule'
	Sentimentalism and people who are over-emotional		Retreat

ways in which as a coach you can work with clients whose resilience has been temporarily lost.

Some other coaching possibilities: getting better at the opposite preferences

Once they understand the subtleties of Type preferences, many clients are interested in learning how to access the opposite preference more readily and skilfully. Explain that such learning is never about becoming equally adept in the opposite preference, but it may involve becoming *good enough*, for instance to enjoy using the opposite preference during their leisure time or when aspects of their work demand it. Table 6.2 offers some suggestions, which of course apply as much to you as the coach as to your clients.

Table 6.2 Practising the use of opposite preferences

When your preference is	. . . and you want to get better at
Extraversion	Introversion, you could try
	restricting the number of contributions you make at a meeting, both in number and in length
	practising listening by learning how to summarize without offering an opinion of your own
	learning simple meditation techniques
	writing down the pros and cons of some proposed course of action rather than talking it through with a friend
Introversion	Extraversion, you could try
	phoning or talking face to face instead of emailing or texting
	initiating conversation rather than waiting for others to make the first move
	increasing your skill and confidence at networking
	challenging yourself to speak at greater length and more frequently at meetings
	making your thinking more visible by explaining how you have arrived at any conclusion
Sensing	Intuition, you could try
	using the table of contents in a book to identify the most interesting bits rather than reading it sequentially
	working with an Intuitive-preference colleague on strategy and consciously looking for how their thinking works

(Continued)

Table 6.2   (continued)

When your preference is	... and you want to get better at
	experimenting with creativity techniques without worrying too much about whether what you produce is 'good'
	preparing for an arts event such as opera, theatre or exhibition by reading the critics' reviews
Intuition	Sensing, you could try
	starting with identifying the known facts when assembling a business case or argument
	during exercise, raising your awareness of every part of your body
	concentrating your thoughts on enjoying the here and now rather than focusing on the future
	extending your awareness of detail in using your five senses – what you can smell, touch, taste, hear, see
Thinking	Feeling, you could try
	in any decision, starting by asking yourself, 'What is the people dimension here?'
	identifying and naming your own feelings in important discussions, especially those involving conflict
	increasing your empathy skills by asking, 'If I were this other person, how would I be feeling right now?'
	praising first and at most length; criticizing less
Feeling	Thinking, you could try
	being direct and straightforward with people when you have to tell them something uncomfortable
	when making a difficult decision, asking yourself what the objective and logical solutions might be
	weighing up whether being kind to an individual may involve a greater unkindness or unfairness to the organization
	stopping yourself from immediately assuming that any negative feedback, however mild, is a personal attack
Judging	Perceiving, you could try
	making fewer lists
	asking yourself, 'do I really have to make a decision right now?'
	giving others advice less frequently; letting them work things out for themselves
	using leisure interests to practise just going with the flow instead of feeling you have to plan everything

Table 6.2 (continued)

When your preference is	. . . and you want to get better at
Perceiving	Judging, you could try
	putting a mental deadline on gathering yet more information in relation to any project – and sticking to it
	a one-day pilot experiment from time to time where you promise yourself you will refuse all tempting distractions and will only deal with your to-do list
	developing a disciplined protocol for daily tasks; doing them first so that you can enjoy staying flexible through the rest of the day
	tackling the temptation to do everything at the last minute
	deliberately scheduling in some contingency time – and leaving it free

Summary

'Good Type development' means in practice that each of us has the potential to develop into the best person we could possibly be. Coaching helps identify what our true preferences are, to become more aware of them and how we are using them. In early life the theory is that we develop our preferred mental Functions (S or N, T or F), ignoring the opposite preferences. In mid-life we begin to develop some facility in the opposites. The Jungian framework helps both coach and client identify where we are on this path and creates a safe space to explore it, whether the topic is leadership or how to manage the stresses of corporate life. Coaching may well include opportunities to explore and practise neglected or opposite preferences.

7 Coaching leaders

Most of my own coaching clients are in leadership roles. Some are already fully familiar with Type concepts, some are not. Type has much to offer in leadership coaching, and in this chapter I explore what this might mean.

When you work as a consultant or a mentor, the client needs to know that you have familiarity and comfort with the technical aspects of their work. Executive coaching is different. So clients in retail do not expect me to have expertise about the supply chain or customer segmenting, though they might rightly expect me to know what these concepts are. Clients in banking do not expect me to understand how LIBOR works. Clients who are architects know that I will be ignorant about the structural engineering aspect of how a building is created. They do all expect that I will understand organization behaviour, know where a leader adds value and what the psychological pressures of a leadership role are.

Leaders as people experts

Views about leadership change according to the time in which the leader lives. In wartime we subscribe to the fantasy of the Great Man, the one individual who can save us when everything seems to be lost. When the economy is booming we want a sunny optimist to tell us that the good times will continue. When the economy is struggling we can become prey to leaders who promise that all the problems are the fault of one group of people (Muslims, Jews, immigrants, a foreign power). In times of moral dilemma we want a subtle thinker.

Despite the millions of words and thousands of books written about leadership, it is sometimes hard to discern a consensus. However, today it seems to me that what we need is leaders who are expert people watchers and interpreters. They need, equally, to understand themselves as fully and expertly as they understand and observe others. In addition, every leader has to balance two equally pressing duties: to create optimism about the future and to challenge complacency about the present. This is where Type ideas can make their contribution.

There is no one personality Type that makes for the ideal leader. This is despite the way that certain Types do seem to dominate when managerial populations are sampled. So in the constantly updated sample of several thousand managers collected by ASK Europe for my book *Sixteen Personality Types at Work in Organisations* (Rogers 2007b), it is clear that ISTJ and ESTJ dominate, followed by ENTJ and ENTP. There are far fewer Feeling-preference Types, with, for instance, ISFP accounting for only 1.8% of the sample, compared with 18.7% for ESTJ.

There are no data on how effective these managers are in their roles. A similar sampling exercise was carried out by Consulting Psychologists Press and reported in Sharon Lebovitz Richmond's book *Introduction to Type and Leadership* (2008). This involved data from nearly 123,000 leaders. Again ESTJ and ISTJ dominated, with ENTJ and ENTP not far behind. Sensing–Feeling-preference leaders were in a small minority. There were striking mismatches here with what is known about the Type preferences of the US population as a whole. We can guess that the reasons might include an organization bias towards data-driven, decisive, logical Types in senior roles who then may recruit people like themselves, along with the possible distaste that some Feeling Types have for what they see as 'toughness' as opposed to harmony. I have seen these patterns in my own coaching practice where managers with a preference for Feeling have often dropped out of large organizations in order to found their own enterprises or else have settled for a pocket of the organization such as HR, Training or Equal Opportunities where they feel more at home.

The overrepresentation of certain Types at senior levels in organizations can be a cause for concern. It can often mean that a dominance of Thinking leaders leads to neglect of the human factors, and it is the human factors that will sabotage any major strategy, unless expertly managed. At the most fundamental level it means that in many organizations, leaders will be managing staff whose Type preferences are more likely to reflect those of the general population and will therefore be very different from their own, leading potentially to much misunderstanding and to botched attempts at change.

This is what was happening for my client Kellie, leading a team composed of six Intuitive Types and one Sensing-preference colleague, the finance director, whose preferences were ISTJ, and all of them, bar one, with a preference for Thinking. This charity had recently merged with another organization as a result of which, for the first time ever, there had been redundancies. A budget deficit meant that there was a need for rapid change in organization culture:

Kellie (charity chief executive, ENTP, leading a team of two ENTJs, two INTJs, one INFP, one ISTJ)

As a senior team we were totally in accord – change had to be quick. We arrived at a new vision easily: it was all about responding to regulatory requirements, streamlining processes, making the 'client journey' quicker and easier. It seemed so simple and obvious. We never anticipated the resistance. People were upset about the way long-standing colleagues had been made redundant; they thought it was 'brutal', just didn't see the urgency, they thought they were already doing a wonderful job with clients, didn't see the need for change at all, why couldn't things just go on as before? When we did a cultural audit it was obvious what was happening. As a team of mostly Intuitive-preference people we had totally ignored the fact that so many of the people we were leading had a preference for Sensing. When we ran a series of events which we called 'Listening Posts' we realized how wrong we had been getting it. Their questions were all about the practicalities, with a lot of anxiety about how our changes might affect the well-being of vulnerable clients as well as what was going to happen tomorrow, not in five years' time!

The truth is that all Types have potential weaknesses as leaders.

Table 7.1 sums up what these might be.

Emotional intelligence and why it matters

As Daniel Goleman's book *Emotional Intelligence: Why It Can Matter More than IQ* (1996) made clear, and as is now widely accepted, it is not enough to be an impressive technical expert in your field because your colleagues will take that for granted; it is emotional intelligence (EQ) that decides whether or not you are successful. Leadership certainly involves conventional intelligence (IQ); without it a leader will always struggle. However, the most recent research on what makes for outstanding leaders demonstrates without a doubt that they also have high levels of EQ. It is not that technical skill and traditional intelligence are irrelevant. It is particularly important, for instance, to be able to do big-picture strategic thinking, to be data-fluent and to have long-term vision. But increasingly it is becoming clear that a high IQ is just an entry qualification. This is especially true the nearer you get to the top of a company. One study compared average senior managers with star performers. Nearly 90% of the difference was due to EQ factors. These are not so-called 'soft factors'. High EQ correlated with performance on measures such as net profit and share price.

Without EQ, it is unlikely that anyone can be a great leader. All coaches will have worked with clients whose careers have suddenly derailed – often with shocking speed – and the cause is virtually always their lack of EQ. They are deeply unaware of the impact of their behaviour on others, or they excuse their lack of self-management because they have little idea of how it is getting in the way of their effectiveness, for instance, that their colleagues will do almost anything to avoid working with them.

Table 7.1 Possible leadership challenges for the 16 Types

ISTJ: may	ISFJ: may	INFJ: may	INTJ: may
Micromanage; seem transfixed by data, ignoring the feelings dimension; automatically reject new ideas and the need for change; look serious and unapproachable; see doom and gloom unnecessarily; be uninspiring as a speaker; lack vision; find it difficult to see the systemic perspective on problems; over-rely on formal processes, neglecting the people side; be too deferential to bosses	Get too fixed on consensus as decision-making style, appearing slow or stuck; expect too much of organization's systems and processes; agree to strategies and plans too readily, stifling own views and then hold grudges; may be over-modest; expect to get appreciation from bosses; becoming self-pitying and stubborn if this seems to be withheld; expect appreciation to be enough in managing team, avoiding giving critical feedback or saying 'no'	Seem dreamy and enigmatic; look too hard for underlying psychological significance in everything; feel that private pondering is enough where vision for the future is concerned; find objectivity and detachment tricky as a boss especially when it comes to giving challenging feedback; wanting to 'help' team members when what they need is direction; apologize unnecessarily; avoid meetings, fail to engage with corporate concerns, do too little networking	See everything as an improvement project even when it is fine as it is; seem remote and unreasonably demanding; lose interest in practical implementation; lack leadership 'presence'; fail to network enough; may ignore boss; underestimate importance of data; fail to pay attention to feelings especially if these seem 'irrational'; show restlessness and impatience with routine and rules; be over-concerned with competence in self and others

ISTP: may	ISFP: may	INFP: may	INTP: may
Overdo improvising; be unable to see the longer term future; confuse followers with constant changes of plan; appear disengaged and cool unless there's a crisis; play politics with boss; lose interest in completing tasks; do too little appreciation; fail to put enough effort into building a team; give too much weight to pragmatism and expediency, leaving others mystified about their personal values	Seem reluctant to lead at all; seem over-influenced by others' views; unwilling to look at underlying causes of problems; get too fixated on the practical at expense of theoretical ideas especially about the future; be too modest; lack visibility; prone to disappearing from public view in a crisis; detest and avoid conflict; easily distracted from goals; may avoid accountability for self and others	Deeply dislike necessary organization alliances and negotiating; overemphasize relationship aspects of team leadership; lack social presence; personalize the slightest criticism; avoid deadlines; be too lenient with others who fail to be accountable while being hard on self; see too many possibilities for the future and get paralysed by indecision; get trapped by perfectionism where own values are concerned	Resist leadership and giving direction, seeing self as merely running a team of equals; impatient with less competent people; over-interested in ideas, logic and analysis seeing emotion as sentimentality; talk too much on special areas of interest and under-contribute everywhere else; barrack from the sidelines without taking personal responsibility; endlessly procrastinate on implementation; squabble needlessly with bosses

(Continued)

Table 7.1 (continued)

ESTP: may	ESFP: may	ENFP: may	ENTP: may
Discount need for longer term vision and purpose, getting too involved in the present; be impatient with analysis and theory; overdo quirkiness and humour including with boss; lack subtlety in managing people who challenge, seeing them as 'whiners'; make decisions too hastily, give blunt and unconsidered feedback; do too much improvising; neglect to build a constituency of supportive peers	Appear too interested in having a good time and cheerleading; avoid strategic planning; see people who challenge as annoying 'doomsayers'; seem glib and superficial; get irritated with quieter colleagues; tempted by the new and shiny; may look materialistic; impatient with necessary processes, taking unwise shortcuts; dismiss deadlines as unimportant; play favourites; avoid self-reflection; have overwhelming need to be liked	Be easily distracted by competing ideas then exhausted by trying to pursue too many at once; vision can get lost in lack of closure; blur personal with professional relationships, hesitating to give necessary feedback; make hasty or extreme judgements about others including boss; too concerned with consensus; overlook practical aspects of own plans or get obsessed by a few of the details	Be impulsive, unfocused, distracted by plethora of own ideas; work messily; fail to get past the brainstorming stage with vision and mission; alienate others with noisy debating style; criticize too casually; get bored with duty to develop poorer performers; seem competitive with own team members, boss and peers; overwhelm with energy and humour; undervalue detail, hierarchy and accountability

ESTJ: may	ESFJ: may	ENFJ: may	ENTJ: may
Be rigid, conveying lack of interest in views of those who disagree or challenge; get stuck on 'efficiency' at cost of people's feelings; over-invest in data and systems as solution to human problems; struggle with conveying long-term vision; have difficulty delegating; may bluster and be too demanding on performance; use 'telling' rather than coaching as default style; get too concerned with unimportant detail, routine and hierarchy	Talk too much; socialize at work too enthusiastically; be too intense; blur personal and professional boundaries; find prioritizing tricky; over-promise and over-commit; get exhausted then self-pitying; avoid seeking feedback on self and get unduly upset if it is critical; avoid tough feedback to others or blurt it out clumsily; dislike change, getting too fixed on tradition; over-value practicality; neglect the skills of logical analysis	Be too fixed on one narrowly idealistic vision, unable to hear legitimate criticisms or consider practicalities and facts; prone to over-optimism; talk too much, failing to notice others' boredom; interpret disagreement with own vision as betrayal; judge people too readily as good/bad; get into tussles with others about who has the 'right' values; try to 'rescue' failing team members rather than to coach or confront them	Alienate with appearance of uncrackable confidence; forget how seniority can cow others; be seen as power-crazed, uninterested in people's feelings; use loud talking as a way of shutting people down; fail to take individual interest in team members; have difficulty delegating and coaching; impatient with people who don't seem to meet own standards; make decisions too quickly, ignoring practical and emotional realities

There are four factors in EQ and all of them have relevance to Type in coaching:

Self-awareness. The theme here is 'know thyself'. It means having a deep understanding of your strengths and weaknesses, triggers and hot buttons. All Type profiles have sections on possible weaknesses associated with each of the 16 Types. Don't skip over these: press the client for examples of how far they recognize these possible pitfalls in themselves. Naming them makes it possible to work on them, especially if you ask what the consequences might be of displaying this behaviour:

> I can look haughty and distant, I know that. The risk is that people won't bring me their concerns. (INTJ)

> People tell me they love my energy and cheerfulness but I know that if I overdo it, it can seem as if I'm a bit superficial and frivolous. (ESFP)

Managing yourself. Knowing yourself only goes so far. If you constantly excuse your own behaviour by saying, 'Oh well, I can't help it, it's just how I am,' you are potentially at risk of derailing because there is a limit to how far other people will put up with failings such as tantrums, manipulation or the kind of high levels of reticence that may suggest aloofness. Personal development always means managing your weaknesses. In the initial debrief, ask the client what their strategies are for managing their known weaknesses and be prepared to add these to the agreed agenda for the coaching:

> I cry too easily – I know it's a weakness. I see it as having 'a leaky face' but it's not doing me any favours at work. (ESFJ)

> I look too passive, inclined to be the observer rather than the participant. People think I lack 'bottle'. I don't, but how do I deal with the perception? (ISFP)

> My 'resting face' looks frowny and disapproving. I try to change it, but it's hard. (INTJ)

Knowing others. A leader with low EQ will tend to attribute all their difficulties with colleagues to 'personality clashes'. I would be a rich woman if I had £100 for every client who has either mentally or actually wrung their hands, giving *personality clash* as the explanation. Type ideas are a wonderful source of quickly conveyed ways to grasp that other people have different ways of thinking and behaving and that they do not do on purpose what you find so very annoying.

'Type is not an excuse' is yet again a reminder that your own Type and those of others never justify the difficulties you have in dealing with conflict. How does the world look from their perspective? Ask your client, 'Given what you now know about Type, what would you guess (or even know) that allegedly tricky colleague's preferences to be? And if that is the case, what does this mean about how you need to approach them?'

Managing others. 'Managing' in this case means dealing skilfully with all the others in the leader's system: seniors, peers and direct reports. It is never about getting others to change: a hopeless task. The only person you can change is yourself. You have no hope of managing others unless you can address all of the first three factors of EQ above. To manage others you need to know yourself, manage yourself, accept and welcome that other people are different, and be able to flex your style accordingly, while never compromising on your own deeply held personal values.

As the EQ concept makes so clear, self-awareness is the foundation. I often discuss that abidingly useful model, the Johari window (Figure 7.1), with clients in leadership roles. The name is not taken from some mysterious Eastern religion but was invented by its progenitors, two American psychology professors

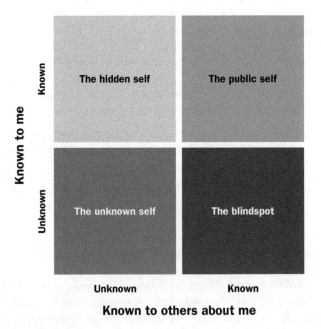

Figure 7.1 The Johari window

called Joseph Luft and Harrington (Harry) Ingram (1955). There are two axes: what I know about myself, what others know about me.

The four-box matrix looks like a window with four panes, hence the name. It assumes that we are all likely to have an unknown self, impenetrable to others and to ourselves; a hidden self where we know about ourselves what others do not; a public self where what we and others know is the same; and a blindspot where others see what we do not. The idea of the Johari window is to expand the area of the public self and to reduce the size of the blindspot and unknown self. You could say that coaching is one of the most effective ways to do this: as a coach you will encourage your client to ask for feedback from others and you will offer feedback yourself. Type is yet another way to achieve the same goal.

I have a private theory that all of us have a version of the blindspot, some cherished self-delusion that has the potential to floor us. Questionnaires like the MBTI can be the means to making these hitherto hidden insights visible:

Rob (retail company, director of merchandising, ENTJ)

Rob's view of himself had been that he was an easy-going pragmatist, popular with his staff. When I ran an in-depth 360 exercise (page 126), this showed him that what he saw as brief, occasional flashes of forgivable temper, mostly out of impatience with himself, were seen by others as frequent, long, terrifying rages aimed at them. Realizing that this was a common trap for ENTJ leaders was startling and comforting. Startling because he literally had no idea that this was what others saw, comforting because it normalized his behaviour as a recognizable pattern, all part of the process of making it manageable. As Rob commented later, 'Now I know why I don't always get what I want. I've been scaring people to death.'

Rachel (telecoms VP, ISTP)

Rachel came to coaching telling me that she thought her personality Type was bound to be ENTJ or ENTP, just like all the other people in the senior team of which she was a member. It was a shock to her to discover that she reported as ISTP and that the profile described her, as she said, 'with spooky accuracy'. In discussion it became clear that the brashness and competitiveness she displayed to her colleagues was an exhausting front that probably deceived no one.

Puncturing these balloons of self-delusion can be a shock, but in the end it is a relief. As one such client said to me, 'I feel I've come home to myself, it's all right to be me but now I've got to make it the best possible version of myself'.

The demands on leaders

So much is now demanded of leaders. If you look through a Jungian lens at what they are told they need, they are expected to be good at everything. So they need to be attentive listeners (I) and persuasive talkers (E); gifted strategists (N) yet know all the detail (S); be tough (T) yet sensitive (F); be able to plan (J) and yet remain adaptable (P). No wonder so many people buckle under the pressure of these unrealizable expectations. Knowing your own personality and its quirks, strengths and weaknesses is the basis of being able to understand and lead others. When you take responsibility for your own behaviour you open yourself to feedback and to vastly increasing your skill in managing the behaviour of others.

In working with leaders from a wide spectrum of sectors and over many years as a coach, I often find myself in awe of what is demanded of them and of how diligent they can be in developing their skills. Leadership is not about privilege and entitlement: the best leaders somehow manage to combine humility with confidence; they do not confuse leadership with the abuse of power and they know that personal development is a lifelong process. These people can find the Jungian approach a perpetual source of energy and inspiration. They understand that it is unlikely that they will become equally good at all eight preferences. Their journey starts with understanding that their first task is to develop excellence in their preferred style:

Daniel (soldier and lawyer, ISTJ)

Being a military leader today is a long way from the stereotyped image of the officer of the past who barked orders and expected instant obedience. Daniel had seen battle and understood how his ISTJ preferences could be a strength. In an emergency he knew that discipline, hierarchy and clarity were essential, but he also understood during our coaching that his instinctive resistance to change could hold him back. He used his strong (Dominant) preference for Thinking as the basis of logical analysis of this and the other issues that he faced daily, making even more explicit his commitment to fairness and objectivity. Daniel's feelings of vague dissatisfaction with his army career became the focus of our coaching and we looked hard at the reasons that could explain it. Daniel made the decision to revisit his early qualification in law and decided to retrain. He stayed in the army and became a judge-advocate, where his ability to absorb a mass of detail and to stay steady under pressure was a considerable advantage. This worked well with the empathy which he had consciously sought to develop as a balance to his preference for Thinking and for bigger-picture thinking (Intuition) as a way of understanding that many of the issues which come to military courts have systemic origins.

Leadership in twenty-first-century organizations is not for the manipulative, the lazy or the arrogant. It can mean taking risks:

Lee (retailer, ENFP)

As the only person with a Feeling preference in an unhappy executive team, Lee found herself constantly used as a bridge-builder between warring colleagues. Her success in leading her own team was all about the strong empathy she was able to develop with her direct reports and the intense personal loyalty she sought from them. In our coaching we looked at how this was most probably becoming a weakness when she placed her team leader role above her corporate responsibility. Her ability to listen without judgement meant that she sometimes excused behaviour that should have been challenged. Learning to value Thinking skills, Lee said, 'felt like walking a precipice all the time. I had to learn to trust my ability to develop objectivity and toughness and to see that closure and firm action were often what was needed for the sake of the business.'

I am lucky enough to work with some clients over long periods of time, not always continuously, but people will re-contact me when they get another promotion or join a new company, knowing that the transition can often be more challenging than it looks during the temporary glow of being offered a new job. The MBTI is a constant touchstone for many of these clients. They work consciously on developing at least some skill in all eight preferences:

Susanne (healthcare CEO, ENTJ)

When I first met Susanne she was running a small hospital in her first chief executive position. Bright, smartly dressed and lively, she might have enjoyed debating theories of leadership with me in our sessions had I been prepared to indulge her – which I was not. She started well in this new role, interviewing staff, visiting wards, observing how patients were treated. She was not impressed with what she saw. She then abruptly announced wholesale changes to roles, processes and structures. She was puzzled that morale took a sharp dip, but this was because like many ENTJs she had positioned herself as the saviour of a broken system, underestimating the amount of time that would be needed to make her changes work and ignoring the feelings of long-serving staff who felt that she had scant respect for their skills and history. A sharp rebuke from her boss and leaked stories to the press created a crisis. Together we looked at the likely cause: overuse of her preferences, with too much talking and not enough listening; too much certainty about what was wrong, without looking hard enough at the data; ignoring the people dimension of her decisions because of her own belief that she wanted only the most competent people around her and that, as she so frequently said, 'they need to think for themselves, I'm not their mother!'

Today, Susanne is in a very senior and influential national healthcare role. She is still a fearless and formidable presence, but watching her at work you would be hard put to see what her preferences are. She has taught herself to be an extraordinary listener. She has consciously appointed people with excellent data (Sensing) skills to her team and knows how to take heed of their insights. She can still see exactly how and why a system should improve, but her ability to manage change has increased exponentially because she knows how to take people with her by appealing to heart as well as head. It has been challenging for her to develop Feeling awareness, telling me at one point that she was 'afraid' of feelings because of a dread that she might be overwhelmed and then be unable to think properly. A turning point for her in our sessions was her realization that she could experience strong emotion but still think and analyse clearly and that her feelings did not need to be rationalized into oblivion.

All of this has taken time, courage, self-awareness and deliberate practice. Sometimes in our sessions she has said to me, 'I'm still essentially an ENTJ, but if I catch myself doing out-of-control ENTJ behaviour,
I ask myself this question: "What would a really skilled ISFP, [her Type
opposite] do here?" That's often enough to stop me in my tracks!'

Leadership coaching is a broader topic than psychological Type, but I find that
Type is invaluable as an adjunct. Look out especially for how it can help with
all these topics:

> *Influencing colleagues*: working with people of the same and differ-
> ent Types. How might your client's and their colleagues' preferences
> affect their style of influencing? (see also page 187)
> *Working with pairs*: for instance, with boss and team member during the
> initial contracting stage where goals are set for the coaching, or later
> if there is conflict which seemingly cannot be resolved:

Simon (ESTJ) and Troy, CEO (ENTJ), hotel chain

Simon's company has just been acquired and he has a new boss, Troy.
Troy is in a hurry to make changes, believing he is running a sleepy
organization that is far too complacent and whose shareholders are
impatient. He has suggested objectives for Simon. Simon sees these as
'commands' rather than suggestions and is indignant – how dare Troy,
the newcomer, assume he knows enough about the organization to do
this when he has only been in it for three weeks? There is an unpleasant
conversation, after which Simon calms down enough to realize that some
coaching help might be useful and asks his coach if she will run a dual
session. In this session ESTJ prickliness about status and the desirability
of gradual change are at odds with the ENTJ wish to sweep everything up
into one major change programme. The coach does not start with these
Type ideas, though she notices how they are playing out in the conversation, but instead facilitates a dialogue about market pressures from
competitors. Here, both Simon and Troy are agreed. About an hour into the
discussion she asks each if they will say a little about how they perceive
themselves to react under pressure and how Type concepts might shed
light on this stress in their own cases. Simon readily describes himself as

being prone to sudden descents into anger if he feels that his efficiency is being challenged, 'I'm like a bull in a china shop' he says. Troy admits to seeming arrogant and know-it-all. The coach reminds them of the different attitudes that ESTJ and ENTJ are likely to have to change and that Type differences are – and need to be – complementary. The session ends in amicable agreement: Troy needs to take more time to learn about the organization he has joined and can do this with Simon's help. Simon needs to embrace the need for change.

Confidence issues: reconnecting with the skills likely to be associated with each Type along with a focused look at feedback from colleagues, noting that how people handle frank feedback varies hugely and that Type can be a major influence on it. So, for instance, Intuitive Thinking (NT) leaders, with their typical investment in competence, can be profoundly rocked by feedback from colleagues which suggests that others find them less than perfect.

Moving from specialist to generalist roles: a transition whose difficulties are often underrated. Look here at what other instruments such as Career Anchors (page 127) can offer alongside Jungian questionnaires. Ideas about Type development (Chapter 6) can be valuable here. How far has the client developed effective use of their preferred mental Functions? How far are they balancing this with effective use of their Tertiary and Inferior Functions (page 56)? This is what can need to happen when a leader moves from being a senior specialist, perhaps running a small team of other specialists, to a more general managerial role which will often include giving primary loyalty to corporate and not specialist concerns. Such moves involve a strikingly different set of skills which are far more concerned with influencing people over whom you have no hierarchical control, communicating with passion and insight in public, giving up time to work on a corporate project which is out of your comfort zone, developing and mentoring more junior people, and leading a team whose own specialisms you may know little about.

Facing career crises such as redundancy or being dismissed. Here Type ideas have multiple applications. Type preferences may help explain why the redundancy or dismissal has happened, often because of under- or overuse of strengths and lack of self-insight. Ideas about Type development may help a client who wants to make a dramatic switch in career, or who has two good job offers and is hesitating about which to choose. There is more about all of this in the next chapter.

Summary

Leadership in the twenty-first century is challenging when in theory leaders have to call on all eight preferences. Type ideas may offer rapid insights, especially into behavioural patterns which involve emotional intelligence.

8 Personality Type and career

Type concepts are valuable when you are working with clients on career issues. While Type concepts are not at all the same as simplistically slotting people into 'suitable' careers, they can often help clients see why one sort of career and work environment might appeal more than another. This is especially true when instruments such as the MBTI are combined with questionnaires that have a specific career focus such as *Career Anchors* or the *Strong Interest Inventory* (see Chapter 10).

The flow of career coaching

A large number of my own coaching clients come with dilemmas and questions about their careers. They may have been made redundant because of an unwelcome reorganization. They may be struggling with the aftermath of a sudden dismissal because of alleged misconduct or be on the receiving end of the harsh pronouncement that a new boss does not see a future for them in the organization. Or the client may be six months into a new job, finding it a whole lot harder than he or she thought it would be, and wondering if they made a mistake in accepting the job. Equally often, there is a sense of low-level misery: dreading Mondays, feeling that each working day is an energy-sapping struggle, watching the clock and longing for it to be going-home-time. Other clients come because they are competing for a new role and want help in preparing for the selection process. Some have been out of the workforce for a number of years because they have had care-giver responsibilities. Many are looking for clarity about what they might do as a next career step. Some have the apparently pleasant dilemma of choosing between two equally attractive job offers.

Career coaching has a natural flow. It will typically start with assessing where you are now: what is it you like and dislike about your current (or most recent) role? What are the facts about your current situation – for instance, employment status, money? Where does work fit with the rest of your life? No career decision is ever made in a vacuum, so this phase of the coaching is about what other needs the client has and that must be honoured. It is usually worth looking at the idea of personal 'brand' and how you convey this in your CV/résumé. There can also be value in discussing job-searching tactics, given that the great majority of jobs appear to be found through the informal job market rather than through advertisements and websites. What works and what is a waste of time? Then there is the whole question of how you present yourself at an interview and how your personal appearance supports your 'brand'. Finally, when the client is successful at interview, there is the issue of negotiating the deal and getting going in a new job.

Mid-life career change?

This process works for people who are already clear about their career paths. It is not so simple for people who are not. In mid-life or later, some people question whether they want to continue on what looked originally like a straight line from one job to another in the same sector or profession. I have worked with many people who were intent on reinventing themselves, so client A gave up a well-paid job in broadcasting to start a charity, client B moved from medicine to freelance journalism, client C left a senior managerial role in the City of London to enter politics, and client D, who had looked all set for a high-level promotion in an insurance company, retrained to become an independent coach.

These transitions are typically slow. Old assumptions are not surrendered easily, new identities emerge bumpily, often after a period of experimentation when fresh skills and interests run in parallel with the old. Some of these experiments lead to blind alleys. For instance, a client whose passion was baking played with the idea of starting a specialist cake company. She took market stalls and sold her cakes readily enough, but realized that the hard physical work, which seemed like fun at weekends, was not such an attractive prospect as a full-time occupation and that operating on the predicted narrow financial margins would not support her family.

Unless you have the privilege of working over a long period of time with a client (and for most coaches this will be a small minority of your client list), your work will most probably have to concentrate on the early part of this cycle: the place where clients are exploring why it is that they feel so restless and uneasy with their current roles. To explore more about how people make profound career shifts, read Herminia Ibarra's fascinating book *Working Identity: Unconventional Strategies for Reinventing Your Career* (2003). She says, and I agree, that these radical changes are never made on the neat, linear plan-then-implement model but rather on the basis of test-then-learn, an iterative process with many stops and starts.

If you meet clients for the first time in the middle of this process, be patient and resist the temptation to assume that there must be a simple, easy answer. Psychologically such clients are in what the writer William Bridges calls the 'neutral zone'. In his book *Transitions: Making Sense of Life's Changes* (2004), he distinguishes three phases of change and transition – endings, the neutral zone and beginnings – making the point that these phases are messy and over-lapping. The neutral zone is the place where it is clear that the old life has ended or is ending but the new has not yet started. While it is disturbing and bewildering, it can also be exhilarating and a time of renewal and learning. Encourage experiment, low-risk training or retraining options, secondments, sabbaticals, volunteering. They can all help:

> *Gabor (ISTP)* was running a mental health team for a local authority and apparently all set for a further promotion. However, he disliked the long hours and dreaded the implications that ever-shrinking budgets were likely to have on his work. He felt exhausted and frustrated by the vulnerabilities of his service-users. He negotiated six months of unpaid leave to experiment with turning his long-standing interest in carpentry into a new career.

> *Sonia (ENTP)* persuaded her employer to pay half the cost of a full-time MBA course. She returned to her employer for another two years while simultaneously planning a software start-up which would supply services to her current employer and to others like them.

> *Martina (INTJ)* had left a career as a pharmacist to become a full-time home-maker for 12 years and at nearly 50 felt chronically unconfident about re-entering the workplace. She spent a year combining informal 'research interviews' with people in her networks with two spells as what she called 'being an elderly intern' for charities in causes that interested her.

The career so far

Most career coaching starts with asking the client for an account of their career so far, why they took each job and why they left, keeping the links with Type somewhere in your mind. These are some helpful areas to explore:

> Which skills did your first job need?
> How did you feel about using and developing those skills?

What were your reasons for leaving that job?
Which skills did you use in subsequent jobs?
How about now? What is the fit between the skills your current job needs
and the ones you pride yourself on having?
What are your leisure interests?

Assessing the current role

I ask clients to make a two column list with me: the pluses and minuses of the
current job. Sometimes the plus side is often woefully short and the minus
side a litany of disappointment and stress. Explore how far this is recent
(rarely) and how far the client believes it is a permanent feature of their jobs
(usually).

Ask 'What would need to happen to improve your job?' It may be that
acquiring new skills and making a different kind of psychological adjustment
is the answer, in which case you coach around how that might happen. But in
most cases, expect the answer 'Nothing!'

When are you happiest and at your best?

Many clients who come for career coaching have one overriding question
in their heads: 'Who will have me?' The more abrupt the disruption to their
career path, the more pressing this question is, but it is the wrong question.
The right question is 'What do I really want?' I ask clients to identify three or
four 'peak moments' from their careers and lives, times when they were 'in
flow', when they felt stretched, happy, confident and were conscious of using
all their skills and qualities. I listen to their stories with their Type preferences
in mind:

Al (Former professional athlete, ESTP)

Al had been a medal-winning professional athlete as a very young
man, but his career had been ended abruptly by injury. Al came from a
privileged background, and his father quickly slotted him into a senior
managerial role in the family business. At 36, Al was miserable and
demotivated, ridden with guilt that he did not feel more grateful to have
a job at all, aware that his colleagues were probably resentful about his
presence, attributing it to nepotism. He struggled with the skills needed by his marketing role and had frequent squabbles with his father.
When I did the 'peak moments' exercise with Al, his scowl lifted as

he described the times when he had felt 'in flow'. The conditions this revealed were:

A sense of fun: jokes and high spirits
Immediate challenge with a tangible goal, spontaneity
Physical activity outdoors
Competing in team sports
Visual pleasure from landscape; especially trees
Sketching and painting
Variety and change every day
Ability to be a trouble-shooter and problem-solver
Tinkering with machinery: repairs, creating ingenious solutions to
    mechanical problems
Working as equals with a team of like-minded people.

More or less everything in Al's then current life was the opposite of these conditions and it was clear that it was not sustainable for him to carry on as he was. Most ESTPs are unlikely to be happy in a job such as Al described where he was office-bound, asked to write long Board papers, obliged to follow a prescribed routine, reach long-term, intangible goals and work largely alone. After flirting with the idea of becoming a fitness instructor or Pilates teacher, Al eventually decided to retrain as a landscape gardener and persuaded his patient dad to invest in starting a small company specializing in high-end town gardens and where Al would lead a small team of three colleagues. This perfect match to his needs created almost immediate success and Al's business has expanded pleasingly. I worked with Al twice during this process, once at the beginning when his frustration had reached melting point and then again three years later when his business was poised to expand dramatically and he felt he needed some leadership coaching.

Assessing skills

When clients have reached a senior level and are therefore likely to be in mid- or late career, they will most probably have a wide range of skills. The issue is often not a lack of skill but how to edit down that wide range. For instance, in their earlier career they may have been a teacher, an accountant, a lawyer, a food technologist, a journalist. They could probably still call on many of those skills if they had to, but do they really want to? Equally, there may be skills that they need or want in order to get or do a new job. I use the like and do well grid, asking clients to fill it in to identify which skills they want to de-emphasize, keep, discard altogether or develop (Figure 8.1). Which skills do they like using, dislike using, and do well or don't do well?

As with Al's experience, above, the Type lens can often explain how and why a job is a poor fit, usually because it demands skill and pleasure in the opposite of the client's preferences. So an Introvert can be driven crazy by the noise and lack of privacy of a large open-plan area; an Extravert may be terminally bored by working largely solo in a cellular office. Someone with a Sensing preference may struggle with a job where strategy is its main focus, an Intuitive-preference person may loathe a job which is all detail and routine. A Thinking-preference client who has to pacify angry customers all day long may feel wrung out by what will seem like pretending, a Feeling-preference person working in a high-conflict team or a job that demands challenging levels of toughness may feel brutalized. A P-preference professional whose job is entirely about planning and deadlines may feel boxed in, a J working in an environment which is all ambiguity could be exhausted by its lack of closure. The more of these psychological discomforts there are, and depending on the skills and aptitudes that the job needs, the worse the fit is likely to be and the easier it will be to define what the client does need in order to thrive.

All clients and all coaching situations are different, but your coaching will need to explore all the options: the default option, staying put and hoping for the best; staying put and seeking some significant change in the job; looking for a new job or a totally new career – remembering to include the needs that are probably associated with the client's Type preferences.

	Skills you don't like using	Skills you do like using
Do well	Skills that the client can use but perhaps with more effort, possibly associated with non-preferred sides of their personality; may be associated with early career choices or paths that have been abandoned	Skills to put at the forefront of a job search because they are probably associated with strengths and with Type preferences
Don't do well	Skills to avoid as they may be associated with the forced use of the non-preferred side of personality or with their Inferior Function (page 56)	Development areas: possibly these are skills associated with a preference that has been suppressed or with one that could be developed in later career as a balance to their actual Type preferences

Figure 8.1 The like and do well grid

For this client it was not about changing jobs but about getting more satisfaction and business success from the job she was already in:

Judith (small business owner, ESTJ)

Judith runs her own accountancy practice. She has a loud, confident voice, likes bold choices in clothing and enjoys her preference for Extraversion. She tells me that she has no difficulty making tough decisions (T) or explaining the labyrinthine legal rules about tax to her clients while wrestling with their tax returns (S). However, she is steadily losing clients to competitors, and the scraps of feedback she has been able to gather suggest that listening and empathy (I and F) are not her strong points, that she does not always think through the longer-term implications (N) of her advice and may be at risk of rushing too soon to conclusions (J – and her Dominant Function is a Judging Function). While this behaviour does indeed fit the predicted pattern (according to Type dynamics theory) of Dominant Extraverted Thinking with a Sensing Auxiliary, Intuition as the Tertiary and Feeling as the Inferior, what is actually more useful is the conversation we are now able to have about getting the maximum benefit from her favourite preferences as well as what it might be like to show more empathetic listening. This may be – and indeed proves to be – a better bet than giving up in despair and selling her practice while she looks around for something else to do.

Similarly, where a client seems to be psychologically 'different' from others in their organization, it is not always the best solution to try copying the style that seems to work for their colleagues:

Jon (diplomat, INFP)

Jon has had feedback from his boss that he is clever, insightful, loyal, is persuasive when working one to one, but 'lacks presence' when in large meetings or in public. This matters as it will potentially hold him back from performing well in a new role where he is running a small embassy – his first solo command. He wonders if maybe he should leave public service and do something else. I hold the Type dynamics theory loosely in my head when I am coaching Jon, and I am interested in his own view of what is going on for him when he has to perform in public. This turns out to be that he sometimes has private disagreements and hesitations about official policy, but mostly he dislikes what he considers to be the dry, rational, policy-heavy speeches he feels he has to give in his representational role. Type dynamics theory does help him understand that Thinking is his fourth/Inferior Function, but this is the one he believes he has to use in public – the style which so many of his Extraverted Dominant-Thinking preference colleagues deploy in these circumstances. This feels inauthentic and uncomfortable to him. Instead of trying what may seem the obvious remedy – getting more at ease with Thinking – in fact we look at how an introverted NF could develop a quiet, compelling, personally based and overtly values-driven way of speaking in public. We look together at the many examples from www.TED.com which show very clearly and attractively how this might be done.

It is my standard practice to explore childhood with clients, including the impact that parents and teachers had on career choice. This will sometimes reveal a profound mismatch, and looking at the implications can be liberating for the client:

Sunita (doctor, ISTJ)

Sunita's parents were part of the callous expulsion of Indians from Uganda in the 1970s. After years of infertility, she was their much-cherished only child. Both parents were distinguished academics. Sunita told me that from her earliest years she had been directed towards becoming a doctor. This was hard work and had involved several exam resits. Now, still labouring to get through the long training involved in medicine, the pressure from her parents was for her to train as a consultant physician in neurology. Sunita was having treatment for depression and had been signed off work for some months. When we had our MBTI discussion, she told me that she longed to be N as all the focus in her home had been about ideas and theories. She struggled with the notion that it was all right to have a preference for Sensing, though it became clearer and clearer that Sunita's interests and skills clustered around this preference. She liked physical detail and was tolerant of routines that might have bored others. She did not enjoy working with patients. She confided that her real ambition was to become a laboratory-based pathologist. Our coaching included discussing how she might achieve this (she did) as well as how to persuade her parents that this was the right and proper path for her to take (in practice much easier than she had imagined).

Sunita's experience is a reminder that in discussions about 'diversity', the usual categories about which we are urged to be aware are gender, age, religion, sexual orientation, disability and race. It is rare indeed for psychological diversity to come onto the agenda, but this is every bit as important. Without awareness, we are all capable of unconscious Type bias. Sunita's parents no doubt assumed that they were acting entirely in her best interests, believing that their own preference for the mindset associated with Intuition was the normal and right way to be.

I have worked with many clients whose parents conveyed similarly unthinking prejudices, for instance a Feeling-preference parent who disapproved of what she saw as the 'cold' approach of her Thinking-preference daughter; a Thinking-preference father who viewed his Feeling-preference and artistically gifted son as 'a bit of a nancy-boy who needs to toughen up'; or Sensing-preference parents who unwittingly made it more difficult for an Intuitive-preference child to pursue his or her interests in the intangible worlds of ideas. I worked recently with a client whose blue-collar parents had strongly urged him to take on an apprenticeship in bricklaying. As he is now a successful architect, he has been able to reassure them that possibly they were right, but not in quite the way they had imagined.

Other aspects of how Type affects career and job search

Type preferences have a part to play in most aspects of career coaching. Quite apart from the crucial questions of personal brand, gifts and skills, the preferences will also potentially affect every aspect of finding a new job.

Extraversion/Introversion will potentially affect choices of clothing and style. A client with a preference for Introversion may baulk at the idea of abandoning her unflattering all-black clothing because her unconscious wish is to be inconspicuous. An Extravert-preference client may propose wearing bold colours to an interview even though she is applying for a role in a company where discreet dark clothing is the norm. Be prepared to offer feedback and challenge when this is what you see.

Extraversion/Introversion may also affect how people like to undertake job-searching. Introverts may have to overcome their distaste for calling people direct and going to see them in person, rather than lurking behind a computer. Extraverts will most probably find it a little easier to spread the focus of their search and may have a wider network to draw on. That being said, Introverts may find it fits their style better to be the person doing the listening in the kind of 'research-based interviews' which often lead to the invitation to send your CV/résumé or to compete for a job.

Clients who have been made redundant and who are still unemployed will benefit from structure and planning in the job search process, but some NP and SP Types may find this torture. With his permission I show such clients the exemplary spreadsheet drawn up by one ISTJ client, which contained every single name in his network, the dates he had contacted them, plus what needed to happen with follow-up activities, with his computer set to give alerts when these were due. The happy-go-lucky process that so many P-preference people instinctively prefer may not serve them well with job search, so discussing how they might adapt what they may see as impossibly constraining could be useful. Equally, J-preference clients may need to be alerted to the possibility of being too rigid and to staying more open to unplanned opportunities when they arise.

Tactics at job interviews

Some of the Types who are more likely to be modest about themselves (for instance, ISFP, INFP, ISFJ, INFJ) can have a visceral distaste for what they may see as 'boasting' in a job interview. Your role here will be to reassure them that licensed boasting of a skilful kind is what is expected in a job interview and to coach them through how it might be done in a way that will feel authentic to them rather than risking losing the job because they will not speak up about their own gifts and experience.

Keep Type preferences in mind when you come to work with clients on other aspects of job interviews. Introverts may lack what head-hunters call 'interview presence' – speaking far too quietly and briefly, not seeing that to some extent an interview is an occasion to play a role: the best and boldest version of themselves.

When I ask people what feedback they have had from previous interviews, some of them will describe having been told that they failed to answer the questions 'properly' or were not appropriately brief and succinct. Almost invariably such clients have ES preferences: they are doing their thinking out loud and get submerged in the detail of their own answers. First I ask them a sample question and set the stopwatch going on my phone so that we can both see how long they are taking (2–3 minutes is ideal). Then I teach them how to use crisp storytelling for maximum impact in their answers, something that N-preference people probably find a little easier.[1]

The impact of early career

When you combine parental pressure with educational and social influences, you can end up with early career choices which with hindsight turn out to be the wrong path. So I have worked with many clients whose best subject at school was maths, who came from modest backgrounds and whose parents had urged them not to bother with all that fiddle-faddle of university but to get out there at 18 to become an accountant, a profession which seems to guarantee stability. Similarly, girls who seem conscientious and well mannered might have been urged by their parents to enter nursing or secretarial work. Often, such clients have found that it then takes much effort to escape what they can see as the straightjacket of their first jobs. Personality Type is helpful in understanding how and why this has happened:

Pamela (HR director, ENTP)

Pamela worked as HR director in a consultancy where she enjoyed the camaraderie and flexibility of the role. What she did not enjoy was the amount of what she called 'pay and rations' work (routine payroll administration, remuneration issues, entry and exit paperwork) that fell to her. A combination of parental pressure, shortage of money and poor career advice had meant that Pamela had left school at 17 and had completed a secretarial training, a quintessentially Sensing qualification. She had disliked what she saw as the boredom of secretarial work, felt she struggled to be more than mediocre in it and saw retraining in HR as a way out, but so far this had just led to yet more Sensing-type work. Taking the MBTI along with a number of other psychometrics showed her immediately that she needed an entirely different role. It is always easier to stay in the sector and role you are in than to seek a radical change, and Pamela followed the sensible route of looking for and finding an HR role where her ENT preferences would be needed and valued. In her case this involved another HR director job but in a bigger company and with notably different responsibilities. Here she became the right-hand person to the chief executive, working on long-term plans for the workforce, on company culture and change, all closely allied to the needs of the business and drawing directly on her ENTP interests and skills. The pay-and-rations duties she quickly outsourced, commenting that it was satisfying to see such work being done by people who were temperamentally suited to it, which, as she said, 'I never was!'

The influence of education

Education has its own pressures. In the first six years, the emphasis tends to be largely on a Sensing approach to learning. The basic skills of reading, writing and maths have to be learnt, and these are largely taught in a Sensing style: step by step, often using helpful routines and strategies. It is possible that early years education tends to attract Sensing-preference teachers for this reason. When education is attacked by politicians, the criticism is usually based on an assumption that it is far too airy-fairy, based on guesswork and other assumed lax and hippyish approaches (Intuition) of the 1970s and 1980s; that teachers should be forced to return to the rote-learning of times tables, phonics and spelling tests, all of these Sensing approaches to learning. You could in fact see the whole UK National Curriculum as an attempt to impose Sensing values on education and 'teaching to the test' (another Sensing approach) as the result of a Sensing–Judging pressure to grade and sort on an increasingly narrow basis. At the secondary/high school education stage, Intuition, especially IN and also INT, becomes gradually more dominant (though this varies according to subject) and in tertiary education is the norm, especially in the humanities with an emphasis on learning techniques such as problem-based learning which stress self-teaching, discovery and project work. Depending on natural preference, this can pose long-lasting difficulties:

Elise (media executive, ISFJ)

Elise had loved all the performing arts as a teenager, but felt she had just about scraped through her degree in Drama and Literature at an elite university. She described failing to grasp what her lecturers needed when they encouraged 'unique' or 'unusual' ideas. As she said to me, she didn't really have any unique or unusual ideas, and was reliant on textbooks and secret coaching from other students. The sense that she was an impostor had persisted into her media career where she had done reasonably well, but at 35 she was stuck, feeling at a perpetual disadvantage with allegedly more 'creative' colleagues. The MBTI was a revelation. It validated her preferences for Sensing and Feeling, explained why she had found higher education so tricky and also why she disliked the overtly competitive (ENT) culture of her firm. In her own view this pointed immediately to a career change and to a job where her SF skills would be needed and recognized. Elise realized that money was not important to her, and found a job at a significantly smaller salary, but a job she loves, as administrator to a non-profit children's performing arts organization.

Summary

Type preferences can be a rich source of data and ideas when clients come for coaching with career issues. Their dissatisfactions with their current role usually have clear links with psychological Type as do their criteria for finding a job which will bring the joy that comes from the full use of their preferences and skills. Education, early career choices and parental pressure may all have played a part in embarking on what has turned out to be the wrong path. Knowing how your Type preferences link with the processes of searching for a new job can also be a valuable source of data for you and your clients.

Note

1   For more on this see my book *Job Interview Success: Be Your Own Coach* (Rogers 2011).

9 Being self-aware: Type on Type

In the end, any tool, whether a psychometric assessment or some other approach, is only ever as good as the coach using it. The real impact in a coaching session comes from the depth of trust in the relationship that the coach and client generate together. As a practitioner you already have some readily available high-quality information here: your own Type preferences and those of your client.

Can you escape your own preferences?

My own Type preferences are INTJ. I like theory. All my career I have been drawn to frameworks and models, especially the ones which simplify the complicated without losing its integrity. This is one of the reasons why I admire the MBTI, because that is exactly what it does. My own interest in and need for competence is one of the reasons why I like the role of developing others and often see strengths in them that they take for granted or miss. I like to focus on what is possible for the future and find it far more challenging to enjoy the here and now. It is a struggle for me to deal with detail: I will obsess over it and also do it badly. My preference for Introversion can mean that I can seem cool, serious, disengaged or inscrutable at first, unless I make a conscious effort: people have to get to know me a little better to see that kindness, humour and generosity are core values for me, even if I don't always live up to such lofty aspirations. My relationships with clients are warm and tend to be very long-lasting. I listen intently and carefully. Like many INTJs, I can appear very certain of my views to the point of seeming arrogant and opinionated, but in practice I am always willing to re-evaluate. I have shaken off the narrow moral judgements on others that I saw all around me in my suburban South Wales childhood. As a boss I had to learn that people crave appreciation and that this must be expressed. The urge to improve everything has to be roped back, especially if it involves saying anything negative, but I am not afraid to challenge if I believe it is in the client's best interests to do so. The feedback I get from clients is that they appreciate my directness and honesty and also understand that it comes from a positive intention: my concern for them. Despite my preference for Introversion I am a good example of the dangers of assuming that Introversion means shyness, as socially I am bold and also enjoy the spotlight of teaching and presenting.

I hope that I have few illusions about the influence all of this has on my practice, but I know that like every other coach, my self-awareness can slip as I default to preferred ways of thinking and being, especially under stress. How my preferences play out in practice can mean that I am absolutely the wrong coach for some clients. A client wanting constant exuberance, noise and jollity, who finds sitting still agonizing, or who learns by taking every topic step by cautious step, a client needing to be bathed in a perpetual stream of warmly extraverted empathy and needing for their own good reasons to do a lot of revisiting of their past would probably find me an extremely poor match. Strangely enough, I am rarely or never approached by such clients.

None of the above should be taken as meaning that I can only work with a restricted range of people. I have worked, I think successfully, with people of all 16 Types and I would encourage you to believe that you can do the same.

Understanding how your own Type preferences affect your coaching

First, look, and I mean *really* look, at the inevitability of your own Type biases. Yes, being pleased and proud to be the Type you are is one thing, but if this actually means a disdain for other Types then beware. How far might you secretly believe that all NFs (STs, SJs, NTs, SPs, ... whatever your own Type preference is) are actually psychologically superior to everyone else? Under seal of absolute confidentiality, here are some MBTI-trained coaches talking honestly about this:

> I couldn't believe at first how, to me, pedantic and rule-bound so many SJs are. I found myself wanting to tell one client, for instance, that punctuality was not and never would be a compelling reason for rewarding someone at work. (INFP coach)

> I can't work with people whose main motivation is money and so many seem to be STJs. (ENFJ coach)

> My worst-ever client experience was with an INTP senior strategist in a big consultancy firm. I was dying to tell him to get over himself, why did he have to talk so much and be so infuriatingly clever-clever? That coaching engagement went nowhere fast. (ISFJ coach)

> I still have to stop myself from telling these gloomy NT Types in government departments that they are already over-achievers, and from blurting out 'loosen up a bit, guys, enjoy yourselves!' (ESFP coach)

> I had one client, ENFP, who was in my view being viciously exploited by everyone in her life, including her husband. I found her passivity

unbelievably annoying – her fear of conflict was palpable. Once I'd recognized what was going on for me here I was able to work with her, but it was a warning. (ENTP coach)

When I work with SF clients I consciously, even now, have to remind myself that the world needs people like this and that they are very good at doing the exact things that I am very bad at. But I find that their need for reassurance can be infuriating, and so many of them seem to spend time constantly apologizing and saying 'sorry'. (ISTJ coach)

Predicting coach–client needs

We can make some broad, general, educated guesses about the coaching style that is likely to be preferred by either coach or client and also the associated dangers (see Table 9.1).

Coach and client together: clash or collaboration?

There are infinite possibilities here. To name just a few:

> *You and your client are Type opposites so what you each want and need are totally at odds.* An unaware NT coach working with an SF client could quickly find the coaching session hitting a wall of puzzlement or openly expressed resistance. The SF client needs overt warmth and immediate practicality, while the NT coach is longing to share their latest reading from the *Harvard Business Review*.
>
> *You are opposites on Introversion and Extraversion.* This is one of the most common problems I hear when I review recorded sessions from coaches working towards their qualifications in coaching. The coach is slow, quiet and thoughtful, the client is lively and loud – or vice versa. This mismatching quickly gets in the way of rapport, limiting the quality of the work that can be done in the session. A coach with a preference for Introversion and who knows how to use silence has a valuable strength, but if it is overdone it can feel to the client like indifference. A coach who loves lively talking can generate energy in the conversation, but if you do too much it can deny the client the space to think: at its extreme, a client whose preference is Introversion may feel hounded by such a coach and simply withdraw their attention.
>
> *You have different preferences on J and P.* The problem shows itself in different attitudes to goals and action plans. The P, whether coach or client, does not want the discussion closed down too soon, or to feel

Table 9.1 Type-generated needs in coach and client

ST	SF
Wants	*Wants*
Concentration on facts; working step by step from the known to the unknown; no time-wasting with trivialities or distractions; reassurance that pragmatic, doable activity will result from the coaching. Respect for efficiency, tradition and order. Clarity about goals and action plans. Dressing the part likely to be important: nothing too casual on either side – this is a business relationship. Straightforward language, avoiding anything that could be seen as 'psychobabble'. Tangible, objective evidence that any suggested approach has worked with other clients. Crisp arrangements about invoicing and meetings, punctuality, delivering on promises about follow-up. Wanting to work with coach/client of equal status	Friendliness and overt warmth; recognition of unique individuality; willingness to bend the coaching rules a little with some light gossip from time to time; evidence about how other clients have benefited told as compelling stories. Detailed discussion mapped carefully about how to implement ideas and understanding that practicality and impact on people likely to be paramount as criteria. Avoiding anything that seems overly academic or that could seem airy-fairy. Focusing on the here and now. Coaching often benefits from using techniques such as role-played rehearsals of immediately challenging situations and often any coaching technique that involves physical activity
Dangers	*Dangers*
Overlooking the importance of feelings between coach and client and in the client's issues. Resisting useful theoretical concepts that could shed light on organizational/human behaviour; over-readiness to see anything psychological as 'fluffy'. Getting snarled up in too much factual detail – e.g. drawing organizational charts, plunging unhelpfully into business plans and balance sheets; focusing on the short term; being too timid about necessary change, seeing only the downsides	Being afraid to confront and challenge; getting into passive resistance; confusing sympathy with empathy. Getting distracted by the need to make the relationship special; getting too personal, allowing boundaries to be blurred. Spending too much time with a problem focus, especially when it involves people not in the room. Overlooking the need to think strategically and longer term when necessary and failing to see the systemic aspects of organizational problems; resisting useful theoretical ideas unless they have some immediately obvious practical application; being too ready to let the other take the lead and then feeling resentful

Table 9.1 (continued)

NT	NF
Wants	*Wants*
Intellectual rigour, suggestions for reading, big ideas, whole-systems thinking. Recognition of personal competence and why it is important. Sessions with changes of pace; surprise, creativity, though nothing too flaky or overtly like commonly held stereotypes about 'therapy'. Appreciates challenge and can give and take tough feedback as long as it is done respectfully. Needs immediate acknowledgement of need for autonomy. Likes to work on large-scale change; unafraid of awkward questions. Values rationality and logic over feelings. Enjoys coaching techniques which encourage long-term thinking, models, theories, links between past present and future and may benefit from being able to read up or think something through between sessions. May resist anything that offers too much intimacy too soon or that appears 'sentimental'	Quick understanding of the critical importance of personal values, building them in to every part of the coaching conversation. Wants to create a warm coach–client relationship built on closely shared values and respect; what you say and what you do must be seamless. Authenticity on both sides is utterly essential – any breach here will quickly bring the coaching to an end. Beginning the exploration of any coaching issue by looking at its impact on relationships and never forgetting the wider social impact. Is comfortable with exploring personal life and links with work life. Responds to vision and belief in the value of development and growth. Expects and needs high degree of emotional literacy. Not fazed by expressing intense emotion in the coaching conversation. Dislikes anything that seems rigid or over-packaged/pre-processed – wants something unique and individual. Rejects detail in favour of looking at big-picture possibilities. May enjoy overtly 'creative' coaching techniques such as drawing, using music
Dangers	*Dangers*
Getting into 'who's got the biggest brain?' competitions between coach and client. Wondering overtly whether this coach/client is good enough for you. Struggles for control of the process (especially NTJs). Neglecting the feelings dimension in discussing any problem, whether the feelings in the coaching room or the feelings involved outside it. Ignoring the detail, facts and data by assuming they are 'unimportant'. Developing plans that are too grandiose to be realized. Seeing a suggestion as an affront to autonomy and competence and rejecting it, even when it might be useful. Forgetting the importance of physical activity – investing too much in the life of the mind. Being too challenging, for instance insensitive with feedback. Not understanding the importance of working in the here and now, e.g. in the coaching itself	Overlooking the importance of facts; developing action plans that are impractical because they are over-ambitious, too vague or set too far into the future. Spending too much of the coaching time on issues of office politics, not being able to get perspective. Caring too much about the harmony of the coach–client relationship and being reluctant to probe and confront. Agreeing too readily that the problems lie with others, overdoing reassurance; avoiding feedback on the coaching and may resist approaches such as in-depth 360 feedback. Getting too carried away with 'insights' that remain unchallenged

too constrained, and may loathe the very idea of 'action plans'. The J can get annoyed by too much flexibility and vagueness. The P may actively dislike words like *goal, plan* and *outcome*.

You have the same Function (column-alike) or Type preference. Here the danger is collusion. Two NFs tacitly agree to assume that ignoring conflict is a good thing and embark on devising elaborate and quite unrealizable strategies to keep everyone happy. Two STs get far too deeply into details and facts, ignoring the emotion involved in any major change project. Two NTJs compete for control of the process, or get too embroiled in fascinating theoretical discussion, taking them away from the main goal for the coaching. Two ESFPs spend too much of the coaching session exchanging enjoyable gossip; two ESTJs share the same blindspots about delegation and never tackle the underlying assumptions which are preventing the client from trusting others to deliver work without micro-supervision.

Responding to difference

I am often asked by beginner coaches, 'What happens if you don't like a client?' My answer is always the same: that it rarely happens now; but far more importantly, that I ask, 'What does my response tell me about myself?' The chances are that I am projecting something I dislike about myself, or fear could be true, onto the client. When you project blame outwards, whether it is the alleged failings of a big institution, or the apparent character flaws of a client, then you can dodge all personal responsibility. Accept that in coaching, as in every other way that we live our lives, that there is no such thing as 'objective reality'. Everything is your own interpretation and the only thing you can ever reliably change is your own behaviour.

Using the MBTI is no different from any other potentially uncomfortable experience with a coaching client. I like Byron Katie's four questions in her simple but profound approach to human change which she calls 'The Work' (see www.thework.com, where you can download a free worksheet):

1 Is it true?
2 Can you absolutely know it's true?
3 How do you react, what happens when you believe that thought?
4 Who would you be without the thought?

So can you be absolutely sure that you know a client is *only* motivated by money? Or can *never* handle conflict? Human motivation is slippery – we are lucky if we understand our own, let alone someone else's. Motivation is rarely just one strand, it is often a combination of many. For instance, a client with a dislike of giving presentations may be motivated by any combination of the following: fear of failure, fear of success, distaste for the scrutiny of so many people, wanting to avoid the feeling that giving a presentation is a form of showing off and therefore 'wrong'. If you feel a diagnosis of a client's motivation coming on, my advice is to lie down until it passes.

The strength and the weakness of the MBTI is that it potentially gives us a quick route into understanding others and an equally quick route into potential prejudice. You can only truly use the MBTI successfully as a coach when you accept that both these routes are flawed. You only ever have the unique individual client in front of you, the unique individual coach.

The value of the Z-shape

To guard against the inevitability of Type prejudice, I find it helpful to remember the simple idea of the Z-shape in exploring any coaching issue with a client (see Figure 9.1; see also how this can work with groups, page 190). This encourages me to visit all four of the mental Functions – Sensing, Intuition, Thinking and Feeling – in that order, with the client. Usually I will draw the diagram for the client, explaining that our natural instinct is to be attracted first and to put far more emphasis on our Dominant Function. I then discuss how far this is true for this client when first considering solutions to whatever problem they have brought to coaching. Using this approach provides a disciplined reminder that any issue worthy of exploration in coaching will involve all four domains.

The distinguished therapist Milton Erikson once commented that there is no such thing as a 'difficult' client, only an inflexible therapist. I profoundly believe the same to be true of coaching. If you find yourself getting indignant and defensive, ask what this says about you rather than believing it reveals how stubborn, defended and obnoxious your client is. Be proud of your expertise, including your knowledge of psychometrics, but be prepared to be gracious, warm and accommodating when clients do not share your enthusiasms as well as being wholeheartedly engaged when they do.

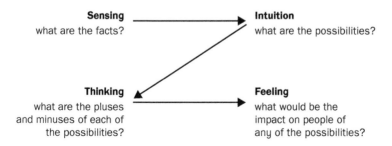

Figure 9.1 The Z-shape approach to problem-solving

Summary

In coaching we are not working *on* the client but *with* them, a human–human engagement. This makes it impossible to be in any way 'objective' because our own Type preferences will always intrude one way or another, but, as with everything else in coaching, self-awareness is the key to managing the interaction. Whether working with people of the opposite, different or the same Type, there will be biases and preferences to remember and accommodations to be made.

10 Using a blend of psychometrics

However much you love the MBTI or other Jungian instruments, it is usually unwise to use them on their own. They cannot predict vocational or personal interests, nor how well we can use the opposite preferences when we need to; they cannot measure emotional intelligence or adjustment. They cannot measure verbal or numerical reasoning. To get into these areas you will need to add other instruments. Just like the MBTI, even the very best of such instruments has weaknesses, along with strengths. In effect, by using several such assessments you are bringing different lenses to bear on the client, each of which will add something unique.

Criteria for choosing

There are thousands of psychometric tools available, many of dubious validity. In choosing what you add to your toolkit, refer to the checklist on page 36 where I discuss alternative Jungian instruments. The same questions apply to any psychometric questionnaire.

I also suggest you consider that it is helpful to find one instrument in each of these categories to work alongside the MBTI:

> *An instrument that measures interpersonal need.* The best of these will allow you to work with the client on identifying how beliefs, values and behaviour originated in childhood and will most likely have profound effects on their behaviour in the present day. Examples here are FIRO-B™ and the Enneagram.
>
> A *motivation, values and drivers questionnaire.* Because much of my own work has a career focus, I like *Career Anchors*, but most of the main suppliers of psychometric questionnaires have something similar to offer. The *Strength Deployment Inventory* (SDI)® can do this, as well as offering other advantages, for instance in use with teams.
>
> A *general personality questionnaire.* These are most frequently trait-based questionnaires. The idea is that if you identify the right groups of behaviours (factor analysis) these will lead you to the inner personality. *The Sixteen Personality Factor Questionnaire* (16PF)™

developed by Raymond Catell is still the gold standard here, though some people would consider that it has been superseded by so-called Big Five questionnaires such as the NEO. In the UK, the *Occupational Personality Questionnaire* (OPQ) is still popular, as is the *Wave* suite. The *Hogan* suite of psychometrics has much to offer as it has the possibility of looking at the 'dark side' – in other words, how our strengths, when overused, can also derail us.

My own top five

In practice your choices will be limited by time, interest and budget. Since I am often asked which questionnaires I use most frequently myself in addition to the MBTI, here they are, in descending order of the frequency with which I use them, with the reasons for my choices.

Fundamental Interpersonal Relations Orientation™ (FIRO®) or FIRO-B™

This instrument, first developed by the research psychologist Will Schutz in the 1950s, gives six basic scores on a 0–9 scale. FIRO-B stands for 'Fundamental Interpersonal Relations Orientation – Behavior'. FIRO-B measures interpersonal need, and the assumption is that all human beings need to belong and to feel significant (Inclusion), to have power and influence (Control) and to love and be loved (Affection). Each of these dimensions has two variants: what we initiate with others (Expressed) and what we want back from them (Wanted). FIRO-B assumes that if you don't like your score or feel it reveals something that disadvantages you, it is possible to change because all behaviour is a choice, even if such choices are often made at an unaware level.

	Inclusion: in or out?	Control: top or bottom?	Affection: close or distant?
Expressed	to include, to involve others in our lives	to influence, to be in charge	to love
Your scores			
Wanted	to be accepted and recognized by others	to be dependent	to be loved
Your scores			
Sum for each			
Overall total			

The FIRO-B gives nine chances to answer the same six questions about where we are in relation to these needs. The scoring is subtle and produces a 10-point scale (0–9) for each area of need. The higher the score, the more likely we are to do the behaviour associated with each need. A low score is usually associated with doing that behaviour more selectively and more rarely.

FIRO as a companion to the MBTI

The FIRO-B is an excellent companion to the MBTI. I like the idea given to me by a fellow coach that the MBTI is the brain's hardware, while FIRO provides the software. This means that your MBTI preferences are most probably laid down either at birth or soon after (scientific opinion is, however, divided on this, so treat this idea with a pinch of salt), while FIRO-B is a response to circumstances, especially your experience of being parented. So a Thinking-preference client may tell you wistfully, 'I'm a softie really', something that shows up as likely in his FIRO Affection scores of 1 for Expressed Affection

Caro (restaurant manager, ISFP)

Caro was in her late twenties and was referred to me by her worried mother, a successful publisher, who felt that Caro ought to be what she called 'making more progress'. Caro had a poorly paid job in a restaurant chain and showed little ambition for change. Did Caro share this concern – and indeed was she even up for coaching at all? Yes, she was certainly up for coaching, and in our second session we debriefed the MBTI, FIRO-B and Career Anchors. These were her results:

	Inclusion: in or out?	Control: top or bottom?	Affection: close or distant?
Expressed	to include, to involve others in our lives	to influence, to be in charge	to love
Your scores	3	2	6
Wanted	to be accepted and recognized by others	to be dependent	to be loved
Your scores	3	3	6
	6	5	12
Overall total			23

On Career Anchors (see below), Caro's number one choice was Lifestyle and her bottom choice was Managerial Competence. Her main hobbies were her allotment, cooking and marathon running. She had taken part in marathons in London, New York and Paris. She described herself as indifferent to money. FIRO-B was enlightening. Her low need for Inclusion suited her just fine and her comment was, 'I'm not willing to pay the high price I see others paying in order to be part of the herd. It would be stifling. I like my small group of friends.' Her low scores on Control explained to her why she had so often taken up the role of 'observer' at work, sometimes at risk of seeming disengaged. She explained that the only person she ever wanted to be in charge of was herself, thus neatly ruling out the career as a senior manager that her mother longed for her to have. Her highest individual and column scores were for Affection, consistent with her preference for Feeling on the MBTI, and she said that she knew she could sometimes be at risk of overwhelming her friends by giving and wanting too much closeness, commenting that perhaps her preference for Introversion kept it under control. Caro was quickly able to clarify her career direction. She decided that a life in the restaurant business was not for her, but that she could develop an interesting portfolio career combined with moving into a rural area. As with so many other clients, taking FIRO-B along with the MBTI and Career Anchors legitimized and speeded up choices she was already on the brink of making.

and 5 for Wanted Affection. In this case what the world sees is a cool person who does not readily disclose feelings, but underneath that cool exterior, he has a longing for love – one which is unlikely to be met as long as he carries on with his Expressed behaviour.

Like the MBTI, there is no assumption with FIRO-B that there are 'good' or 'bad' scores, only consequences, and that behaviour can be learnt which overcomes any of the potential disadvantages of any one score. There is some research on correlations with the MBTI, but most of these correlations turn out to be weak.

FIRO-B can be an annoying questionnaire to fill in as the items are phrased in slightly odd ways and appear to be repetitious – and they are. However, it only takes about 10 minutes to complete, so any irritation is short-lived. It is difficult to 'cheat' as each item is uniquely scored. Many coaches find FIRO-B tricky to interpret as there is an art in seeing how each score has a subtle impact on all the other scores, and it takes persistence, practice with willing guinea-pigs and perhaps the help of a more experienced practitioner to get to the true value from the whole profile.

FIRO-B: Summary

Licensing and training necessary?	Yes
Ease of interpretation?	Moderate–difficult
Other materials available?	Yes, but they are relatively sparse in number. Existing materials include an explanatory booklet co-authored project by Waterman and Rogers (1997) plus other materials available in the UK from OPP and in the US from CPP
Upsides	Apparent simplicity conceals complexity. Cuts quickly to essentials of client behaviour. Considerable potential for client insights, including resolving to change dysfunctional behaviours; excellent partner to MBTI
Downsides	Irritating to fill in. Clients with medium scores may say, 'So what?' Coach needs considerable practice to be able to interpret whole profile confidently and skilfully

360 degree feedback

The danger in coaching is that you and the client sit together in private under seal of confidentiality and you hear the client's version of events. Depending on the client's temperament and levels of emotional intelligence, what you hear could be rounded, self-aware and shrewd. Or it may not be. Getting other people's observations into the frame is always critically important, and one of the best ways of doing this is through a so-called 360 feedback process, where other people's views of the client become part of the picture. Usually you will need at least eight respondents to give a valid picture, and they need to be a mix of direct reports, peers and the boss. Sometimes it is useful to ask clients/customers for their feedback as well. The client gives his or her view of themselves as part of the process.

From once having been a rarity, most large organizations now administer 360 feedback for their middle-level and senior staff. The most usual way to do this is through an internet-delivered questionnaire which goes to a selection of staff nominated by the person who is the focus of the report. The report itself gives bar charts which show how self-ratings compare with those of boss, peers and direct reports for each item on the questionnaire.

Problems with 360 questionnaires

Questionnaire-based feedback is cheap, simple to administer and certainly better than no feedback at all, but it is limited in its scope. The rating scales (typically 1–5) may be used by different people in very different ways, so the air of scientific objectivity may be spurious. People can get tired of filling in lengthy questionnaires, and by the time they get to item 70 may just click on any old thing to get it over with, especially if they are completing questionnaires for a number of co-workers. The true value is in the narrative comment, but my experience is that this is virtually always cryptic and conveys headline statements only, leaving the subject of the report baffled – and sometimes indignant – about what is meant, thus making it easy to sidestep the messages.

The 360 interview alternative

Instead I recommend that you consider using an interview-based 360 process. This follows the same principles as for questionnaires: between eight and 12 feedback-givers nominated by the client, a promise of non-attributable confidentiality and a focus on development. You can ask the client for areas which they would particularly like you to explore as well as the standard leadership categories which will be on your list of topics anyway. You carry out the interviews by phone. Each interview takes a minimum of 20 minutes, and respondents are probed for examples of the person's behaviour, strengths and weaknesses. I do not claim that this methodology is perfect. It depends on interviewers keeping an absolutely open mind, being able probe skilfully and to write the report in a way that the client can hear and understand. It is inevitably impressionistic, so the client needs to be able to trust your judgement here. Also, it is far more expensive for the client than an internet-delivered questionnaire. However, I believe that the extra cost is more than justified by the hugely enhanced value it delivers.

Talking to an unseen, neutral listener/interviewer encourages the candour which it is difficult for most of us to convey face to face to a colleague. Respondents can be probed for behavioural examples of what they mean by their assertions. It is rare for the report to contain material that is totally new to the client, but it is common for the client to be startled by the vehemence with which people hold their views, and also sometimes to be gratifyingly surprised by the elements that their colleagues admire, many of which the client could have been taking for granted.

How to do this interview-based feedback is beyond my scope here as it is more demanding and complex than it may look on the surface and most coaches benefit from getting some training in how to do it.

Links with the MBTI

This is a wonderfully direct way of linking the client's preferences on the MBTI with their actual behaviour as seen by others. It is a way of linking each of their preferences, strengths, blindspots and underuse of the opposite preference with how others see them. It enables you to have a Type development conversation (see Chapter 6) of a much more realistic and focused sort:

Roberta (consultant, ISTP)

Roberta had recently changed from a specialist professional role to one where she was managing 30 staff in a large consultancy firm. Soon she was the focus of complaints about her 'coldness', the alleged brusqueness of her style, her propensity for shutting herself in her office and refusing to answer her phone, for constantly seeming inconsistent by changing her mind, and for seeming to enjoy what her colleagues dubbed 'scheming'. Preferences for ISTP can explain some but not all of such behaviour, and Roberta's instinct was to defend herself by denying that she displayed any of the downsides associated with ISTP and to complain that in any case her job lacked the excitement she had experienced as a trouble-shooter in her previous role.

Debriefing her 360 feedback was challenging for her and for me, but it enabled her to understand that her behaviour could indeed be perceived as 'cold' if preferences for Introversion and Thinking get out of hand and are not balanced by developing some skills in Extraversion and Feeling. The upside of a Perceiving preference is flexibility, but this needs to be reined in by knowing when a decision has to be made. The plain evidence from the 360 interviews was that Roberta was getting a lot of this wrong. Combining the MBTI with 360 feedback and with *Career Anchors*, where her top Anchor was Technical Competence and her bottom one was General Managerial Competence (see below), was enough to convince Roberta that she and her employer had made a mistake in offering her a managerial role. The remainder of the coaching was about how to manage her preferences for Introversion and Perceiving more skilfully as well as about how to double back on her career path.

360 feedback: Summary

Licensing and training necessary?	Sometimes, but not if you do the interview version, though note that training can help
Ease of interpretation?	Depends on skill of coach, potentially easy

Other materials available?	No
Upsides	Focused, tailored, potentially frank and hard-hitting as well as reassuring; gets past client denials
Downsides	The interview-based 360 is more challenging to do well than it seems; expensive for the client, so only really likely to be commissioned for the most senior people

Career Anchors

There are some good career- and motivation-focused instruments available. For instance, I sometimes use the *Strong Interest Inventory*, a classic questionnaire which is well researched and constantly updated, with a history stretching back decades. However, I prefer the simplicity in terms of administration, cost and feedback of *Career Anchors*, based on the work of Edgar Schein. Schein suggests that in any career and life, there is one overriding motivator or driver. This driver is supported by core skills and underpinned by deeply held values. These connect to our life purpose, whether or not we are conscious of this link. Discovering your core driver/motivator is therefore critical. It can help clients in three ways. First, it can help in identifying what direction they should take after a forced career move triggered by redundancy or dismissal. Secondly, it can clarify where they should look when they have a growing feeling of dissatisfaction with current life and career. Thirdly, it can help in deciding which path to take when they have what look like equally attractive options.

Schein calls these core motivators *career anchors* and he identified eight of them. Taking the questionnaire enables you to rank the eight in order of their priority for you:

Technical/Functional Competence: being an expert, valuing your subject expertise; getting recognition from peers

General Managerial Competence: taking delight in managing and organizing, valuing promotion, enjoying the wheeling and dealing of organizational life

Autonomy and Independence: no-strings working and private life, self-recognition the only important thing; the natural freelancer

Security/Stability: long-term predictability even if at the cost of lack of excitement

Entrepreneurial Creativity: creating a new business, risk-taking, retaining control of products and services

Sense of Service: wanting to improve the world through dedication to a good cause

Pure Challenge: conquering the impossible, whether a physical or a moral challenge; winning against overwhelming odds

Lifestyle: integrating your career with your whole life, balancing everything but putting quality of life first, valuing the flexibility that allows for personal time

These 'anchors' help distinguish between what Schein calls the 'external career' – the actual jobs and qualifications that form the externally visible stages in a career – and the 'internal career'. The internal career is driven by the values, talents and motivators that we all have. Schein suggests that there is always one core driver that represents the foundation of who we are: something we would never willingly give up.

I find Career Anchors invaluable as a partner to the MBTI. The MBTI does have career applications, but this is not its main focus. Linking the MBTI with a specifically career-directed instrument can increase the value of both:

Josh (entrepreneur, ENTJ)

Josh worked with his wife in a family consulting business and hated it. He felt constrained by targets, even the ones he had personally devised. The MBTI showed him that he had an itch for autonomy, long-term thinking, leadership and competence, but it was Career Anchors that brought the moment of real enlightenment. His top choice was Entrepreneurial Creativity. His bottom choice was Technical/Functional Competence, the very motivator which his then current job required. He left and started a number of successful businesses in his own name, selling some, buying others and over a period of ten years became a multi-millionaire.

Maggie (lawyer, INFP)

Maggie recognized herself immediately as an INFP but as a senior litigator in a criminal law practice was constantly uneasy about her work and felt constrained by her informal role of being conciliator between so many apparently rivalrous Intuitive Thinking (NT) colleagues. The MBTI showed her that working for an organization she believed in was important, revealed her strong preference for Introversion and also suggested her liking for harmony. When she took the Career Anchors survey, her number one choice was Sense of Service, a motivator that was at odds with the role she was required to play professionally. She trained as a mediator, switched to a firm specializing in immigration and human rights cases and felt immediately at home, not only with the purpose of the new practice but also because she was able to use her preference for Introversion to the full with the opportunity to work one to one and in depth with individual clients.

You can buy Career Anchors in book form, one volume of which is aimed at coaches/facilitators, or the questionnaire can be taken online. The questionnaire is short, with only 40 items. The books are self-contained with full descriptions of the anchors. You don't need special training or licensing.

Career Anchors: Summary

Licensing and training necessary?	No
Ease of interpretation?	Easy
Other materials available?	Yes, three short large format books
Upsides	Simplicity, speed, low cost
Downsides	May strike some clients as simplistic; coach needs to take care that client understands that there is subtlety beneath the apparent simplicity

The Thomas–Kilmann Conflict Mode Instrument (TKI)

Conflict of one kind or another is unavoidable, whether it is a minor disagreement with your teenage daughter about the shortness of her skirt or a full-on battle for control of an organization. How you manage conflict, and its benign cousin, influencing people effectively, is one of the perpetual challenges of managerial life. Show me a manager who has a wide range of subtly effective influencing styles and I will show you an outstanding boss. To my mind it is the skill of influencing and managing conflict which distinguishes the leader who will shine from the one who is good enough. I observe that most of us have a rather limited palette of influencing skills and could benefit hugely from broadening it. I find the Thomas–Kilmann Conflict Mode Instrument (TKI) a simple but effective way of doing this, along with the MBTI.

Kenneth Thomas and Ralph Kilmann developed the TKI, calling the two axes Assertiveness (how much you act to further your own interests) and Co-operativeness (how much you put the interests of others first). The questionnaire consists of 30 pairs of statements in a forced-choice format. From this it will show you how much you use one of the five styles (see below and Figure 10.1), against a large norm group of other people.

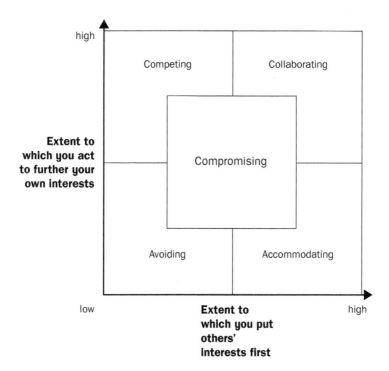

Figure 10.1 The Thomas–Kilmann Conflict Mode Instrument

This questionnaire has a number of attractions. It is short. The framework is sensible and overtly recognizes a dilemma that any of us encounters dozens of times a day: how far we look out for ourselves against how far we meet other people's needs. It links directly to managerial dilemmas such as:

When do I need to insist on having things done my way?
When should I be delegating?
I value collaboration but the other person doesn't seem to, so now what?
In formal negotiations, for instance about salary or conditions, how long should I hold out for what I think is right for the interests I represent?
When is it better to step away from conflict completely?

The five styles

Competing is about having your own way because you think it is right, ignoring the needs of others. The plus is that there are times when direction is essential – for instance, in an emergency or because there is an ethical dilemma where insisting seems like the right thing to do. The minus is potentially undermining others and creating resistance.

Collaborating combines being assertive and being co-operative. It means trying to meet the needs of all concerned, including your own. The minus is that the other party may not put the same value on collaboration as you and you might therefore be wasting your time.

Compromising is the give-a-little-gain-a-little style. It works when there is a need for a pragmatic solution that will save face for all concerned. The risk is of giving away too much too soon.

Accommodating means putting the other person's needs first and may be an effective way of developing others. The downside is of appearing to lack impact and authority.

Avoiding is about stepping away completely, a good style to use when the struggle is pointless, a bad one to use when the situation needs decisiveness or a more consensual approach.

The value of the TKI is that it assumes that there is a time and place for all five of the styles and also that most of us will tend to overuse one or two of the five possible styles and underuse the others. This makes a refreshing change from some managerial grids of the conventional sort which tend to assume that the top right quadrant is the desirable place to be, in this case the style the TKI calls Collaborative.

Links with the MBTI

Executive coaching clients will frequently present with dilemmas around influencing and managing conflict. Their MBTI profiles will be able to suggest a great deal about how they typically approach influencing and also how they like to be influenced themselves, for instance, that someone with a preference for Sensing will expect to hear facts and figures and to be taken step by step through a proposal. We might expect a client with a preference for Feeling to be more accommodating than one with a preference for Thinking. But this cannot pinpoint how any individual's style will play out. The focus in the TKI on all five styles being acceptable is a good match to the MBTI's focus on all 16 Types having strengths. As a coach you can ask the client for examples of overuse of a style as well as coaching them in how they might develop and make greater use of the style they use least:

Raj (senior doctor, ISTJ)

Raj had recently been promoted to clinical director in his hospital. His ultimate ambition was to become a professor of emergency medicine. He saw the clinical director role as a useful step along the way. But nothing had prepared him for its managerial aspects and he was struggling. Raj smiled as he read the ISTJ profile, agreeing that he could be a stickler for accuracy, record-keeping and traditional reporting procedures. At first he found it literally unbelievable that Intuitive Thinking Types (most probably large numbers of his colleagues) were unlikely to put the same value on such processes. Raj struck me as charming, serious, quiet but forceful; he exuded compressed energy along with a certainty that his own views on the world were correct. He was having difficulty sleeping and reported being 'super-stressed a lot of the time'. His opinions on his colleagues seemed to be that they were either what he called 'excellent fellows [sic], good eggs' or 'basket cases', a good example of how ISTJs can be prone to rather digital thinking. I soon had the impression that Raj was over-relying on a directive style and suggested that this might be the case. The idea of there being a variety of styles was new to Raj and he readily agreed to take the TKI, saying he was 'mystified' by why his colleagues didn't just do what they were told, which to him was the obvious and sensible thing.

Results for Raj on the TKI

Mode	Low (25%)	Medium (75%)	High (100%)
Competing			87
Compromising		49	
Collaborating		42	
Accommodating	22		
Avoiding	6		

These results suggested that Raj was over-relying on Competing and underusing all four of the other styles. His experience as a consultant in emergency medicine had possibly encouraged his natural bias to this style as in the emergency room it is indeed often useful to give crisp clear orders and to expect others to obey. An ISTJ can enjoy hierarchy especially when in a senior role themselves, and the STJ preferences can sometimes mean unawareness of or lack of interest in the bigger picture. ISTJs can often find it difficult to delegate, something Raj agreed he found challenging. In talking through his typical day, it became obvious that 'delegating' to Raj actually meant asking someone to do a task and then standing over them while they did it. We could have got to this point with the MBTI alone, but the TKI was quicker, pointing out how radically he was probably underusing Accommodating. We also discussed the use of the other three styles, including when his least-used style, Avoiding, would be appropriate – for instance, in pointless railing against some of the battles that common sense suggested he just could not win.

Thomas and Kilmann have published research on correlations with the MBTI, and you can find it at http://www.kilmanndiagnostics.com/interpersonal-conflict-handling-behavior-reflections-jungian-personality-dimensions.

Thomas–Kilmann Conflict Mode Instrument: Summary

Licensing and training necessary?	No
Ease of interpretation?	Easy

Other materials available?	A facilitator's/trainer's guide
Upsides	Simplicity, speed, low cost. Paper version of questionnaire contains all the interpretative material you need; can also be done online
Downsides	Forced-choice format annoys some clients

General trait-based instruments

There is a wide range of excellent instruments available here. Choose from Wave (Saville Consulting Wave®), the OPQ, the 16PF®, the NEO, the Hogan suite of surveys and many others.

Differences between trait and Type theory

Trait-based instruments are constructed differently from the MBTI. They work on the basis of identifying a number of factors which are assumed to be universal pointers to a basic underlying feature of human personality. The OPQ and the 16PF are good examples of this type of questionnaire. These are *normative* instruments where raw scores produce weightings. Scores (often *sten* scores, that is, *standard ten*, 1–10 scales) are derived from a norm group.

These trait-based instruments are a valuable and different way to look at human personality from Jungian instruments. For instance, they can legitimately be used to assess people for jobs as part of the selection process.

The main differences between the MBTI and trait-based instruments are shown in Table 10.1.

The Big Five

Seventy years of research into human personality has produced a broad measure of agreement about how to measure traits. Meta-analyses have produced five main factors, sometimes known as the Big Five. These are:

Openness
Conscientiousness
Extraversion
Agreeableness
Neuroticism

The factors are easy to remember with the acronym OCEAN. The Five Factor model is based on a combination of the work of several psychometricians, but like most other psychometrics it is still based on self-report, so as with others, can be open to falsification.

Table 10.1 Differences between trait and Type theory

Trait theory	Type theory
Based on assumption that human personality has characteristics that present themselves in differing quantities – e.g. persuasiveness, detail-consciousness	Based on the concept of preference on a bi-polar scale and present in the person from birth
Measures how much of a trait a person has	Sorts on the basis of thinking style
Very low or very high scores are part of the interpretation	Extreme scores only measure how clear the person is about their preference
Assumes that behaviour is caused by traits	Assumes that behaviour is the result of underlying preferences; there is more emphasis on thought processes than on behaviour
Makes judgements about the person's mental health, competence	Type is independent of competence or mental health; no pathology is measured
Often assumes that there is a 'golden mean', so to be in the middle is a strength	Assumes that to be in the middle is interesting but does not necessarily imply strength and could be a disadvantage
Assumes change can take place if people consciously work on a particular trait or group of traits	Assumes change is a lifelong journey of 'good Type development'
Assumes that it is possible to be good at everything	Assumes that it is better to accept and develop your areas of strength, probably associated with particular preferences first, then to develop some skill in their opposites
Frequently used for selection and assessment	Should never be used for assessment, only for development

Openness

Openness means being open to new experiences and ideas, appreciation for imagination, valuing the arts and creative expression.

People who score highly on openness enjoy novelty. They tend to value autonomy and uniqueness and are attracted by the arts. They are interested in empathy and accepting of the quirks and peculiarities of others. Too much openness may look like being unconventional for its own sake, while people who score low on openness may prefer the conventional, the tried and tested. There are many occupations where lower scores on openness are an advantage, for instance, willingness to follow rules where breaches of such rules would endanger life. In some cases such people can seem wilfully dogged, reluctant to embrace change and narrowly conservative.

Conscientiousness

Conscientiousness is a tendency to do your duty, follow the rules, take care with your work, plan and value achievement.

People who score highly on conscientiousness put work before play. They will seem reliable, thorough and persistent. They will be even-tempered and able to stay cool despite being provoked, focused on whatever tasks they or others have set. A high score might suggest being rule-bound even when rules need to be bent, and of being seen as dry and dull. People who score low in Conscientiousness may be more likely to give way to their impulses, to value spontaneity and fun and to be willing to find ingenious ways around the rules. If this goes too far they will seem eccentric, unreliable and unpredictable.

Extraversion

Extraversion, also spelt 'extroversion', is about liking to talk, seeking excitement, activity and involvement with others. If this goes too far, they may annoy others with constant talking, or by being noisy and restless. More introverted people value privacy, time alone and the chance to think before speaking. At the extreme end of the introversion spectrum, such people may lack confidence or their silences could be interpreted by others as unexpressed criticism.

Agreeableness

Agreeableness is being tolerant, accepting and collaborative rather than guarded and antagonistic towards others.

People who score highly on Agreeableness will most probably take a positive view of human nature and will value harmony. Scoring at the highest end of agreeableness may mean they take an over-optimistic view of life or try too hard to be liked. At the other end of the scale, a low score on agreeableness would suggest that such people believe others cannot be trusted and that they intend you harm. They might be guarded and prickly, easily sparked into jealousy and suspicion.

Neuroticism

Neuroticism is a tendency to be emotionally labile, to give way quickly to unpleasant feelings, to be prone to anxiety and depression and to experience criticism as a personal slight.

People with high levels of Neuroticism can be at the mercy of their emotions. They may feel anxious, beset by small challenges which others would take in their stride. Everything feels overwhelming, extreme, and these feelings can be long-lasting. At the other end of the spectrum are people who are emotionally stable and calm, able to take personal responsibility. Their calmness does not necessarily mean they experience happiness, and in fact too much calm can seem unnatural.

Links with the MBTI

Research has shown moderate levels of correlation between the Big Five factors and the MBTI: openness correlates with S-N; conscientiousness with J-P; extraversion with E-I; and agreeableness with T-F. Step II of the MBTI may also give some implied correlations with neuroticism, but this is beyond the stated intention of the original instrument.

Where trait-based instruments can add value

Because the MBTI cannot tell you how much or how little of a preference you use, and is specifically not designed to measure adjustment, it can be helpful to add instruments that do just that. No human being is 100% perfect, and in fact it is clear that even the most senior and distinguished leaders have obvious flaws which are the counterbalance to their many talents. Trait-based instruments give clients the chance to assess themselves against others: do I have too much or too little of a particular trait or am I at the mean (average)? Here are some of the circumstances in which I have found such instruments useful:

> The client has had feedback which puzzles or upsets them. They may be anywhere on the spectrum of acceptance–denial, but they are asking, 'What does this say about the real me?'
>
> Where a client is denying personal responsibility for some adverse incident and blaming others, a trait-based approach may help them see what they have, possibly unwittingly, contributed to the problem
>
> Having had such feedback, the client's next question is 'Can I change?'
>
> The client is focusing on the negatives of performance and cannot separate the specifics of some incident from the underlying issues, let alone see that the apparent negatives may be balanced by strengths that they are taking for granted or under-valuing
>
> There is a danger of overusing a strength to the point where it becomes a handicap and potential career derailer.

Most of the major trait-based psychometric questionnaires will produce a computer-generated narrative report. This is helpful to the client – and to the coach. However, the quality of these reports is highly variable. I find that with some such reports, whatever the quality of the individual paragraphs, there is just too much information. Sometimes the documents are unattractively bulky with complicated instructions, endless bar charts and dozens of pages of 'development suggestions'. When clients bring along past reports, for instance from assessment centres in which they have taken part, they will often confess that they never have really read the material, it is simply too dense. I remember one such report, let's say it was from a fictional instrument called the Leadership Insights Motivational Optimizer, LIMO for short, which has 250 items and takes at least 55 minutes to complete. The client heaves it out of his bag, saying, 'It's called LIMO and it needs one. I took one look and decided I'd read it on the plane going home from the course, but it weighed a ton and I shoved it in my suitcase and never looked at it again.'

Nevertheless, trait-based instruments can often add detail and clarity to a client's dilemmas:

Deborah (charity chief executive, ESFJ)

Deborah is fiercely committed to her organization, has a reputation for imposing high standards and for her practical concern for the charity's users/clients – in other words, very typical of an ESFJ leader. She is admired for the rigorous way she has introduced an innovative fund-raising scheme. She came for coaching because she reported that her stress was becoming overwhelming. She had tried all of what she called 'the obvious', which in her case meant telling herself not to be 'silly'. This is an adapted extract from the trait-based questionnaire I used with her:

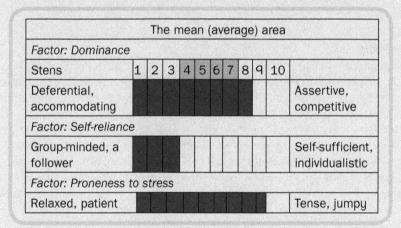

The mean (average) area		
Factor: Dominance		
Stens 1 2 3 4 5 6 7 8 9 10		
Deferential, accommodating		Assertive, competitive
Factor: Self-reliance		
Group-minded, a follower		Self-sufficient, individualistic
Factor: Proneness to stress		
Relaxed, patient		Tense, jumpy

Deborah's results show a common conundrum. If you look at the first two factors in her results you will see that she scores at sten 8 for asser-tiveness, so this is someone who likes to have her own way. Yet at the same time her scores on self-reliance suggest that she is highly group-oriented and likes to be a follower. At first sight this may seem fine, and in some ways it is: she likes to be consensual yet also enjoys develop-ing policy and giving people direction. However, the chances are that she may strike others as inconsistent. On the one hand she is competitive and assertive, yet on the other she seems highly dependent on what others think. Clients like this may sometimes over-rely on approaches to persuasion that can seem manipulative. Deborah described perpetual anger and frustration but believed her anger was well hidden by her mask of 'niceness', though the mask was actually a lot less effective than she thought. The third factor, measuring how stressed someone reports themselves as being, showed her to be a tense and driven individual, a perfectionist who found it hard to relax. Discussing all of this in coaching will enable her to see that she needs to manage her emotional state more effectively if she wants to get good work out of her team. The interesting contradictions revealed by the trait-based instrument neatly encapsulated the whole of her dilemma around stress and led us back to her childhood where the message she had received from over-protective and domineering parents was that she was expected to be a high achiever and yet at the same time it was her duty to do as she was told and that her own needs mattered little. Looking as objectively as possible at all of this was the beginning of finding effective ways of managing her stress.

The Hogan suite

You might also like to consider the Hogan suite of instruments. There are three: a classic personality instrument (the Hogan Personality Inventory); a motivation and values questionnaire (the Motives and Values Preference Inventory); and one that is unique in my view, the Hogan Development Survey (HDS). The latter is an assessment of the individual's strengths and of what Hogan calls 'the dark side' – the ability we can all have to overuse our strengths so that they become weaknesses. Weaknesses are best seen as failed attempts to manage others. So the legitimate levers of power, influence and relationship become attempts to intimidate, control and seduce. The report includes observations from colleagues, and this gives it additional usefulness:

Fabian (TV producer, INTP)

Fabian had recently been through a development centre in his broadcasting organization. At only 24, Fabian had already become a senior producer, making programmes which attracted attention and controversy. His visual flair was outstanding. By 30 he had been promoted again, but his employer was having doubts about him as there were hints that other producers were wary about working with him, despite his undeniable brilliance and quirky humour. Then a misjudged prank created embarrassment for his employer with the broadcasting regulator, though Fabian's own view was that the importance of this episode had been absurdly magnified. His boss suggested coaching. Fabian's low expectations of coaching included 'mystical jargon and general rubbish'. After some candid mutual contracting where I asked for his commitment to the process and promised him that mystical jargon and general rubbish were not what I thought I delivered, we agreed to work together. I offered him the MBTI and FIRO-B. At the session where we were to discuss the results, he brought along his Hogan report from the development centre, on which he claimed he had never had a debrief: 'This chap just thrust the report into my hand and I saw it was all psychobabble so I didn't read it.' His total scores on FIRO-B were only 16, with a zero-zero on Affection (see earlier in this chapter), suggesting someone with a low need for closeness and interaction unless on his own terms, and he agreed that INTP on the MBTI described him perfectly.

Fabian's 'dark side' jumped out of his Hogan report. Compared with the norm group, his scores for mischievousness suggested someone who had a high need to stir things up just to see what would happen, defying even sensible rules and likely to be an impulsive risk taker. On the imaginative scale he was again well into the potential danger zone, with the score of someone easily bored and who had no idea that when imaginativeness got out of hand it could become eccentric and disruptive, demonstrating poor judgement. Although these connect with certain INTP characteristics – for instance, the playfulness, intellectual gaming and love of black humour that many INTPs can have – there was no way we could have arrived so quickly at this conclusion from the MBTI alone.

From seeing coaching as a contest where his object was either to overwhelm me with charm and zany humour or to annoy me with provocatively inappropriate behaviour, Fabian changed his views. Adding Career Anchors revealed that his number one anchor was Autonomy. We spent three further sessions working on what it would mean in practice if he were to decide to run his own business. Within a few months Fabian had left conventional employment and now works successfully as an independent film-maker. I am still in touch with him and every now and again I get an email typically saying some version of 'Still looking for that non-boring executive producer who can stop me from embarrassing myself and help me rein in my dark side!'

Licensing training is usually essential with trait-based instruments, and some are also expensive to administer. A simple version of a Big Five questionnaire can be taken online and for free (www.personal.psu.edu/j5j/IPIP/ipipneo120. htm). If you are new to this area, this would be a good place to start, using yourself as your first guinea-pig.

It can be difficult to choose from the plethora of excellent instruments in this area. Take advice from other coaches about what they find adds value, but remember that their approaches and yours and their work and yours may be different. In making your choice, always take the instrument yourself first and have a full feedback session from an experienced practitioner. If you get no value from an instrument yourself, why would you suggest it to clients? Remember, too, that the best of these instruments are, like the MBTI, highly revealing about your own needs and your style as a coach, all of which has to be factored into the coaching process.

Trait-based personality questionnaires: Summary

Licensing and training necessary?	Yes, usually, but some are freely available on the internet
Ease of interpretation?	Moderate–difficult
Other materials available?	Usually a technical manual; some providers run regular workshops as top-ups
Upsides	Complexity and subtlety. Many focus on leadership. Best instruments reliable and valid with serious research behind them. Can give hard-hitting detailed behavioural insights which other approaches cannot match
Downsides	The best are demanding to interpret; it is easy to miss subtleties, interactions and results which go beyond expected correlations. Computer narratives are often clunky. Training can be expensive – you need to know you will make enough use to cover investment costs

A word about the Enneagram

I first met this approach to human personality through a friend who was an enthusiast for it. I was a little wary as this friend is renowned for her fleeting flirtations with Eastern religions which often seem to involve fasting, temple bells, incense and tents in lonely places. However, I enrolled for what turned out to be an excellent course given by Helen Palmer, one of the outstanding Enneagram teachers of our time. The Enneagram allegedly originated as a Sufi approach to personality, positing nine basic human Types ('Enneagram' means nine-pointed diagram).

The entire event was skilfully, subtly and orally taught – there was no questionnaire. The Enneagram hits hard at soft spots and delusions. It assumes, as does the MBTI, that every personality Type has strengths and weaknesses. Unlike the MBTI, it starts with the weaknesses, but roots them in the helplessness of childhood experience. It had a powerful impact on me. As an Enneagram Point 3, I recognized my need for performance and the primitive link I had made as a child: that love depended on competence. The overt links with religion (there is a Jesuit connection of sorts) was highly off-putting to someone like me with no religious beliefs, and I recognized symptoms of unthinking devotion in some of the people I met through the course. But I have never found any other approach so powerful in linking our defencelessness as children and the strategies we adopt in order to make ourselves feel safe, to the way those self-same strategies can floor us as adults.

Today there are questionnaires – some are free and you can take them for yourself. Try googling *Enneagram questionnaires* to see what comes up. Yet I have never recommended a single one of these questionnaires to a client. Why? Essentially because to do it justice would, I believe, take more time and involve more willingness to engage in an extensive exploration of childhood than there usually is in coaching senior executives – the core of my own business. Instead I use the Enneagram as a private benchmark. I make my own guess about the client's Enneagram preferences, checking it out and revising it through questioning and exploring their childhood recollections and the impact these seem to have currently. Just occasionally, very occasionally, I might send such a client an Enneagram profile to read and ponder. If you are interested and intrigued, I recommend you get some training and see whether you can make the same or some more specific use of the Enneagram in your work.

Other instruments and approaches

There are literally thousands of questionnaires. You could spend serious amounts of time and money learning about them and getting training – but would you use them? Only you can decide what the priority is for you. For instance, with the rise of 'positive psychology' have come some attractive questionnaires which concentrate on strengths rather than weaknesses. Many of these are free or cheap and do not need extensive training and licensing. For instance, you can take Martin Seligman's *Values in Action Inventory of Strengths* (VIA-IS) survey free on the internet (http://www.viacharacter.org/www/). There is also the Gallup organization's questionnaire, the *Clifton Strengthsfinder®*, and the British instrument, *Realise2*, which offers a clever take on strengths by distinguishing between innate gifts and those skills which you have acquired and which may therefore take more effort. I do not routinely use any of these questionnaires, though I have colleagues who like them a lot. The *Belbin® Team Roles* questionnaire is widely used in the UK, and clients may tell you what their preferred roles are. Belbin is a useful way of identifying informal roles in teams, and there is now a version which gives other people's views of the client as well as their own. There are also some questionnaires which claim to measure emotional intelligence, the best of which involve asking colleagues to rate the client, along with a self-score.

Summary

There are many dozens of other excellent instruments available and which cover a whole range of topics such as motivation, skills, stress levels or emotional intelligence. Using more than one will also give you more than one chance to make an impact on the client. The ones I like and return to again and again because I see their value in the coaching process are the ones I describe in this chapter. They sit well with the MBTI and each has something unique to add which the others lack.

Each client and coaching engagement is different. Use the MBTI as your foundation but aim to combine it with at least one and possibly two, three or more other instruments, depending on what the client's situation seems to need, how much time you have for the session and what your own levels of expertise are. There is no one right way, but adding at least a little psychometric variety will give power and impact to your coaching with the MBTI.

11 Working with groups: where Jungian instruments add value

Few coaches work exclusively one to one. More commonly you will combine individual with group work. This chapter looks at the case for using Type indicators such as the MBTI with groups.

Groups, boards and teams

Consultants, coaches and facilitators have been working with groups for the best part of 80 years, but there is a confusing array of words used to describe what we do. In the early years of organizational consulting this was described as a 'group intervention'. Then, because managers frequently took their teams away from their normal places of work in order to encourage what was intended to be literally a fresh perspective, these events were referred to as 'off-sites', especially in the US. Thanks to a well-known railway advertising campaign in the UK in the 1970s where a cheap return rail ticket offered the promise of a fun day out, such events are still commonly described as 'awaydays'. The cynical in organizations will consciously draw on this original meaning to assume that they are 'jollies', meaning that they are legitimized as a way of getting out of the office but that no real work is ever done. More recently, as one-to-one coaching has taken hold in organization life, the phrases 'team development' and 'team coaching' have been used, in this case to describe a longer process than a one-off event with a facilitator. Team coaching implies that the team and its boss commit to working over a period of time with a coach, meeting for regular workshops to extend and review learning. It is also common for boards of directors or trustees to commission board development or board evaluation processes which may have some of the same flavour.

What is a 'team'?

A group may challenge the idea that they are actually a team, and they may be right. This does not mean that you should refuse to work with them, but it will make a difference to what work you do and how you do it. So a 'team' may actually just be a working group of random departments who happen to report in to the same boss for administrative convenience. I was once part of such a group myself, and my colleagues and the functions we led had little in common. However, since our mutual boss was the ultimate purse-holder, we did regularly have to make difficult collective decisions about the use of resources, so to my mind that made us a team. Over a period of a few years we grew to like and respect each other, thanks to the time our boss wisely ensured that we spent together at off-site events.

One way of looking at this question is to ask the team where they fall on a graph which plots levels of ambiguity in the team's environment against their levels of interdependency, on a 1–10 scale (Figure 11.1). The more the levels of ambiguity and the levels of interdependency meet somewhere in the top right quadrant, the higher the stakes and the more the group can potentially benefit from team coaching.

The stressful life of the corporate executive

Corporate life is stressful. Senior people are exposed as never before: their salaries are public knowledge, their slightest indiscretion can be captured on a smartphone, long hours are the norm. International travel can absorb

Level of ambiguity		1	2	3	4	5	6	7	8	9	10
	10										
	9										
	8										
	7										
	6										
	5										
	4										
	3										
	2										
	1										
		Level of interdependency									

Figure 11.1 Ambiguity and interdependency in teams

prodigious amounts of time and energy. One of my coaching clients reckoned that he had flown from London to California and back ten times in as many months. Another client crossed Europe twice in a typical week, and it was no surprise to me that she constantly mislaid essential objects such as her money, keys, passport and, in one instance, her carry-on suitcase. Ambitious people may compromise their personal lives in exchange for the elusive benefits of more status and more money, often only to find that their families can no longer bear their physical and psychological absence, so the promise to themselves that 'at some time in the future I will relax with my family' turns out to be flimsy. They spend more time with their colleagues than they do at home, and the work team may become in effect their family. Yet these relationships are most often flawed: colleagues disappoint, betray, leave, are less than truthful.

This is why working with teams can be so valuable, where it is their process rather than their hard data that is the focus. It is a place where they can talk about what is rarely talked about openly and collectively: how it feels to be in that team and how it might need to feel better in order that the team's work can be done to a higher standard.

Why coach a team or group?

There is a strong case for undertaking this work. A human group can be full of intelligent, conscientious people and yet find that, mysteriously, it constantly sabotages itself. The reason is that our innate need for autonomy rubs directly against our innate need for leadership and direction. In literally every group there is a dance where this contradiction is played out minute by minute, though much of it may be well hidden. When we have a leader we like and respect or sometimes whom we fear, we will trade some of our need for autonomy for the apparent security that going along with the leader and the rest of the group requires, though often at high psychological cost.

Our need to avoid isolation is also overwhelming. We are a herd species and cannot survive alone for long either psychologically or physically. This explains why so many members of groups tolerate a group climate which is gruelling and dysfunctional. No one wants to be the first to name the misery in case everyone turns on this brave person and tells them that they are wrong in their criticisms. Isolation is a fearful punishment. This is why it is so common in groups for everyone to do what no one really wants.

The metaphor of an iceberg is often used to explain what is going on. An iceberg has more under than above the surface, and it is what is the under the surface that has the power to do the damage (Figure 11.2). In groups what is visible, known and acknowledged is that the group has a task to accomplish: getting from A to B. There are roles to play, milestones to manage and budgets to spend along the route.

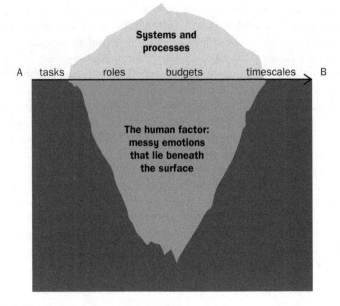

Figure 11.2 The iceberg of organizational life

Under the surface lie all the human emotions: happiness, joy, rage, disappointment, jealously, love, shame, loyalty – and hundreds more. Many clients have told me with utter sincerity that they leave their emotions at home. Alas, if only ... The human emotions often cannot be acknowledged; what we try to do is to solve the problems that they create with a system, so if there are problems with performance, let's create an appraisal system; problems with regulating the flow of money, create a finance system; problems with how we promote people, create a talent-management system. All organizations need systems, but systems alone never can or will manage all the messiness of human emotion. There is a high price for failing to tackle such issues and there is an abundance of research showing that a team with a positive climate is also likely to be a team whose performance is outstanding.

It is at the point where an astute boss understands what is going on here that he or she may commission some kind of skilled intervention from a coach or consultant.

The pattern of problems

The problems fall into recognizable patterns:

Roles and responsibilities. Groups and teams evolve over time. What was once clear may have become fudged and messy. Newly appointed people may appear to have roles that overlap with the roles of people who are well established. In other cases everyone may assume that someone else has a particular responsibility but in reality no one has it:

Rob's team in a telecoms organization had six members. All had migrated to their roles from different departments and two reported on 'professional' matters to another director, but what constituted 'professional' was not well defined. The head of communications was often in dispute with the head of strategy about priorities, and the head of finance saw herself as primarily ensuring that legal requirements were met rather than offering Rob advice on the financial implications of the team's decisions. Low-level boundary disputes were sapping the energy and goodwill of this team.

Purpose. What are we here for? What would be missed if we were not? These seem like basic questions, yet the moment you look below the surface of many groups or teams you will find that disagreement and confusion reigns:

Jenna and Sandie had started their internet-based clothing company in classic style from a spare bedroom. The company had grown rapidly to the point where they were employing 50 staff on two sites. A short-term cash flow crisis forced the founders to look again at why they were in business. Jenna wanted to make as much money as possible in as short a time as possible in order to sell the company and sail around the world on the proceeds. Sandie was far more interested in creating a name for herself as a designer of high-quality classic clothing. She was satisfied with much slower growth and did not want to sell the company.

Relationships. No team or group can be successful without high levels of openness and trust between each and every member of it. Trust is the result of a climate where it is safe to be vulnerable, a rare phenomenon, since for multiple reasons, most of us become expert at defending ourselves and concealing our vulnerability. When this happens, suspicion, jealousy and hostility are the result. The symptoms are faux politeness in meetings followed by private whining in corridors with the people we perceive to share our opinions. There is a profound fear of exposing discontent, for instance about the quality of leadership, the behaviour of certain individuals or naming 'the elephant in the room' – something so large and dominating that although everyone knows of its existence, it can never be spoken about openly (Figure 11.3).

> Helena was the newly appointed CEO of a retail organization. Individually people had spoken to her about their belief that one member of this team had been in a sexual relationship with the previous CEO and that this was what explained this woman's allegedly over-privileged position. It was widely believed to be 'impossible' to raise this issue because it was too delicate, too unprovable and too 'dangerous'. The distraction and underground hostility created by this belief were preventing Helena from establishing her leadership or from focusing on the challenges that the organization faced from competitors.

Values and 'ground rules'. What rules, explicit and implicit, govern how the group behaves when it is together? In my own work I have frequently seen teams where striking amounts of dysfunctional behaviour are tolerated, and where, for instance, people arrive late for team meetings and leave early with perfunctory explanations and apologies, where almost every member of the group literally has their head down during meetings because they are openly texting or writing emails, or where people return from executive team meetings to their own teams saying that they have no respect for their peers or boss and have no intention of implementing any of the decisions that have apparently been made:

> Niall's team of analysts deeply dislike their weekly meetings. If they can, they will find thin excuses not to attend. Decisions are made and action points agreed but it is rare for any deadline to be met. When members of this group meet people in other parts of the organization they are openly critical of decisions they have themselves endorsed.

How a team coach helps

No systems or imposed 'rules' can resolve any of these common scenarios. Nor is it likely that a single intervention, for instance a one-off meeting with a team coach, will instantly improve deeply rooted ways of behaving which, in

Figure 11.3 The elephant in the room

Source: Chris Radley.

many cases, have taken years to become ingrained and are taken for granted as immutable.

Human behaviour in groups will only change when everyone sees the consequences of continuing as they are against the benefits and risks of doing something different. This takes time, skill and effort to plan and embed. People sometimes ask why such teams cannot sort out these problems for themselves: why do they need a coach? Teams do sort the problems themselves, but in most teams the boss is as much part of the problem as every other member of the group, and when we are part of the problem we lose perspective. It can take an outsider with no long-term past with the team and no long-term commitment to its future to see what is going on and to risk naming it.

The benefits of Type questionnaires in team coaching

A single session using the MBTI, or any other Jungian psychometric, is never the whole answer, since there is no one intervention of any kind that can be an instant solution. Mostly what a team coach does is to facilitate discussion based on the topics that are critical to the team's future success.

However, there are enormous benefits in using a personality Type questionnaire such as the MBTI with teams and groups as one part of this process. First and most critically, its strengths-based approach makes it an extremely safe way to explore differences. The firm pronouncement from you as their facilitator-coach that there are no better-than or worse-than Types is just the beginning of allowing people to see the value of difference and that it is all right to be yourself. As Patrick Lencioni writes in his excellent book *The Five Dysfunctions of a Team* (2002) it is the so-called 'soft skills' that matter to performance:

> it is only when team members are truly comfortable being exposed to one another that they begin to act without concern for protecting themselves. As a result they can focus their energy and attention completely on the job at hand rather than being strategically disingenuous or political with one another ... The costs of failing to do this are great. Teams that lack trust waste inordinate amounts of time and energy managing their behaviours and interactions within the group.
> (p. 196)

Self-awareness is the foundation of the emotional intelligence that all teams need. The advantage of the Jungian approach is that it allows people to acknowledge their weaknesses as well as their strengths and to opt for change by taking responsibility for the way their own behaviour may trigger unwanted responses in others.

The unconscious and unspoken assumption is many teams is that everyone needs to be the same. To discover the massive benefit in being psychologically different is hugely liberating. It can also be challenging to discover how lopsided a group has become:

Jonathan was proud of the diversity in his team of 12. There were five women and seven men, and ages ranged from early thirties to early sixties. The team included a gay man and a gay woman. But when he looked at their Type table he and they had a shock:

ISTJ	ISFJ	INFJ	INTJ ******
ISTP	ISFP	INFP	INTP
ESTP	ESFP	ENFP	ENTP
ESTJ	ESFJ	ENFJ	ENTJ ******

This team was diverse in a number of desirable ways. But psychologically diverse it was not. Every single member had preferences for Intuition, Thinking and Judging. This group stared thoughtfully at their Type table until one person broke the silence. 'It explains a lot, doesn't it?' she said. 'It explains why we're brilliant at dreaming up strategies and absolutely terrible at implementing them. And it explains why there's so much rivalry – we all want to be the boss! And it may explain why our people think we're far too critical and demanding!'

Type theory suggests that in a team where people share a number of their preferences it will be initially easy to get along together. But, as with Jonathan's team, it is likely that they will share a number of blindspots as well as strengths and also possible that they will unthinkingly appoint people just like themselves. A team where people are psychologically different will probably take longer to get on good terms but there will be enormous added value in the range of outlooks and skills that they are likely to bring with them.

Unlike trait-based questionnaires (page 135), Jungian instruments lend themselves to group exploration and discussion. Capsule portraits of each of the 16 Types can be read easily and quickly; the table itself can be displayed on a flip chart, as a slide or even represented on the floor. There are many dozens of possibilities for exercises and activities, none of which can be accomplished with trait-based questionnaires.

One of the greatest pluses of using Type approaches is that its language becomes embedded in the organization. It gives people tools for managing difference. This CEO describes how he has taken Type concepts into several of the organizations where he has worked:

> I was first introduced to the MBTI as a sceptical young manager but quickly realized how useful it was. As I got promoted, I instigated regular awaydays with the teams I was leading as a way of reviewing our work and our relationships. The MBTI was always somewhere on the agenda. Slowly it became part of our managerial vocabulary, a useful code. So, for instance, although of course you can't use it for hiring, it was taken for granted that in thinking about a senior vacancy, the HR director and I would discuss what kind of profile we needed ideally and would phrase the job spec and ad in a way that would appeal, say, to an ESTJ. If members of the team were in some kind of dispute, it was perfectly normal to ask them to see it from the perspective of their differing Jungian preferences.

When is the right time to introduce psychological Type?

Using the MBTI or some other psychometric is never my first resort in working with a team as their coach. There are many situations where I do not use psychometrics at all. It would rarely be part of the first intervention, and I strongly advise against making it the only intervention. The exception would be a situation where as an expert interpreter of the MBTI you are invited in as a guest facilitator by another coach/consultant:

Maya accepted a invitation by Jed, a trusted colleague of long standing, to do a half day on the MBTI. Jed was in the middle of a substantial team coaching programme with the UK executive team of a utilities company. Previous topics had covered strategic direction, team climate and team roles. Now, Jed felt that they were ready for some work on relationships with the MBTI as the introductory phase, but he also felt that his own knowledge of the instrument was relatively superficial. He briefed Maya carefully on all of this and was present as her assistant during the event. Maya had joined them for dinner on the previous evening and stayed on in the afternoon so that she could add any observations which would deepen insights that the group had gained during the morning.

Similarly, I will refuse invitations to make the MBTI the single and only piece of work that a boss wants to commission with their team. Instead I will see it as one possible part of a longer piece of work.

The contracting conversation

No sensible coach would ever take on a one-to-one client without a conversation about what the client wants and needs, matching this with what you as the coach feel you can provide. In the same way, there is a contracting conversation with the client who wants to commission some work with their team or group. Some clients are reluctant to spend time and money on solving serious problems that have taken years to develop: one such client told me despairingly about his team and then suggested that all its problems could be solved in a single day with the MBTI in the morning and some brief discussion about roles in the afternoon. As with individual clients, you need to be prepared to say no if what the client wants and what you offer seem to be miles apart. This needs to be a frank conversation whose topics will typically cover:

What's the issue that's triggered this need?
What do you believe are the underlying causes?
What's the cost of doing nothing?
What have you already tried?
If things were going along well, what would be happening?
What are your own ideas about what would help?
What do you need from me?
What's the timescale?
What's the budget?
How much time are you prepared to devote to the process?
How much risk are you prepared to take?

Interviews

Never agree to meeting the team or group for the first time at the first workshop. Ask instead to interview everyone individually and on the basis of non-attributable confidentiality, telling people that your aim will be to produce a short report which identifies the main issues. Keep the questions simple. I like these:

> What's your formal role in this team?
> What's your informal role (e.g. bridge-builder, ideas person, risk assessor, clown, challenger)?
> What's going well?
> What's not going so well?
> What big challenges lie ahead for this team?
> Ideally what would you like to see happen to change things for the better (or build on what is already going well)?
> What's standing in the way of that happening?
> If you could wave a magic wand, what one thing would improve how you do your own work?

The report you produce should be written in such a way that everyone you interview can read it and without their confidentiality being compromised. In your debrief with the commissioning client, now is the time to discuss where the MBTI or other Jungian instrument can play a part, plus possibly some other psychometrics such as the FIRO-B or the TKI (Chapter 10), depending on what your interviews have revealed. Each situation will be different, as these coaches' descriptions point out:

> Relationships were at all-time low in this team. I suggested we spent the whole of our first day discussing my report where all of this was laid bare, and doing some work on what a well-functioning team would look like, sound like and feel like. It was a two-day residential workshop. There was a surprisingly convivial evening, perhaps because so much that had been unsaid for so long was now being expressed. The next morning I did a Type workshop where people explored what their preferences meant and confirmed their 'best fit Type'. Then in the afternoon we built on that to do some work on influencing and conflict, drawing on Type ideas.
>
> (Coach working with a team in the fast-food sector)
>
> The most vital topic to tackle first was their enormously varying ideas on purpose and strategy. Their sector was in a chaotic state of change because of the digital revolution. This work revealed differences that could not be smoothed over, and within a few months two

members of that team had decided to leave. After that there was work on roles. But then the relationship issue came fully into focus. This is where I suggested spending a whole day on both the MBTI and FIRO-B. The advantage of this was that by this stage there was a high level of liking and trust between me and the group and I had also observed a lot of what I assumed, correctly, to be Type differences as seen in their behaviour.

(Coach working with a team in the logistics sector)

This team had felt badly scarred by resentful accusations about 'bankers' that were still widely flung around even after the recession was over. We had already done workshops on the external challenges, what their stakeholders needed from them and what their overall objectives for the next two years should be. It was important for them to build an explicit set of values for their team, and for every-one to endorse them by spelling out agreed behaviour. I found the MBTI to be extremely valuable here as we were able to start from a vigorous debate about what each of the Function-alike Types (ST, SF, NF, NT) valued about work. This produced a much more rounded list than the usual platitudinous stuff that I have seen so often in other organizations.

(Coach working with a team in the finance sector)

Good practice

If you plan to use a Type instrument with a team or group, the same prin-ciples of ethical practice apply as for individuals (Chapter 2) but with a few extra tweaks. Taking the questionnaire should be voluntary, but in saying this I am mindful that group pressure makes it hard to refuse. To make refusal less likely, it is essential to email everyone in advance explaining what the instru-ment measures, that there are no right/wrong answers and how any results will be recorded and stored. If people have concerns about who will have access to their results, you need to be able to assure them with confidence, because you have discussed it with your commissioning client, that such results will not be used for any other purpose than development, and that they will know what the limits of confidentiality are. I will always explain how I plan to explore the results, reassuring people that there will be ample opportunity for discussion and questions, ending my email by encouraging people to text or call me in advance if they have concerns.

The absolute ideal is to offer every participant a one-to-one session in advance where they get skilled feedback and come to the workshop already confident about their profile, including any questions and uncertainties they may have about it, but constraints of time and budget may make this impossible. If so, then assume that you need a half day to allow people to experience the preferences in action and to come to their own conclusions about their own personality profile.

The safer people feel about taking the instrument, the less likely it is that they will refuse to participate in the event itself, but if they do, just acknowledge their reluctance and reassure them that revealing their Type or taking part in any of the exercises is always voluntary. It is good practice to emphasize this – for instance, if you ask people to write their names on a Type table. Sometimes people hang back because they are unsure about what the questionnaire has revealed, even if you have asked people to place themselves on a Type table after a whole session of activities and exercises. If so, accept it and move on.

Always have materials for each participant to take away. If people have taken the questionnaire online they will have an individual profile to read and bring along. This does not meet the need to see quickly and clearly what their colleagues' profiles suggest, so it is essential to have booklets and other back-up materials available, for instance a copy of your PowerPoint slides. Sometimes a client will succumb to what I can only see as a false economy here. I politely backed out of one project when the commissioning client told me that her organization had a set of my books on the MBTI, but that these were for 'borrowing only' and had to be returned after the workshop. I keep the price of these books low, but I was not prepared to give copies away and she was not prepared to budge, so despite my best efforts at negotiating, that was one piece of work that never happened.

Depending on the size of the group, it is a good idea to allocate observers for each small group exercise. Their task will be to look out for the process patterns: who spoke, how they spoke, what vocabulary they used. This shares the responsibility: you no longer need to be the sole point of interpretation and pronouncement.

Keep any exercises short: 6–7 minutes is usually the maximum and often 5 minutes is enough. The reason for this restriction is that the other preferences will start to influence how people behave. Where people are uncertain about their preferences, reassure them that this is fine and consider inviting them to be observers of whichever exercise you are running. You may sometimes have groups that seem unwieldy because they are so big. When this happens, divide them into parallel smaller groups; five or six people is usually plenty, or, depending on the circumstances, double them up so that, for instance, you have two groups of Thinking-preference people rather than one. Where someone is the only representative of their Type or preference, offer to work with them yourself, confining yourself to open-ended questions and letting them do any reporting back.

The point of exercises and activities is threefold. By taking part, people can clarify what the preference means. Type preferences are essentially about thinking patterns, but the activities and exercises can help people understand how such patterns influence behaviour. Finally, the exercises are vivid and people remember not only how they behaved themselves but also what others did:

> This was a very large group of managers on a training programme. We did an exercise where we were in Type-alike groups and I was with five other INTJs. The instruction was to create a picture on a flip chart which represented our Type. We squabbled vigorously about what the instruction meant and we could not agree. Nor could we agree on what to draw. In the end we each drew our own picture on separate pieces of paper. Heigh-ho! INTJ: driving need is for independence! That image has remained with me for twenty years and I remind myself of it weekly when I work with other bosses in my company, which includes many other TJ Types and at least two other INTJs.

The team coach role

In doing this work, I remind myself that I am working from coaching principles just as much as I am with individuals. Your expertise lies in your knowledge of human psychology and how it applies to groups. You are doing both more and less than 'chairing', a different role which is about decision-making by someone who shares accountability for what is decided. You will not live with decisions, so you have the luxury of being independent. You are making it safe for people to talk about their feelings, you are able to keep discussion divergent when it matters, stopping consensus developing too soon, creating the right blend of challenge and support, confronting blockages, offering feedback, suspending judgement. You are neutral but not neutered. It is not your role to solve the group's problems: only they can do that. You are creating a climate of challenge, warmth and acceptance where it is all right to express uncertainty and to ask for help. Your role is to generate learning: nothing else matters. You will need all the many skills of facilitation as the foundation of everything you do, alongside your expert knowledge of whichever psychometrics you are using.[1]

'Ground rules' that help

In working with groups it has become standard practice to ask the group to suggest 'ground rules'. Invariably these are the familiar clichés of openness, honesty, feedback and 'what's in the room stays in the room'. Yet you only have to be an hour or so into the event to see that these 'rules' are mostly being ignored. Instead, I now usually suggest that the best ways of making productive use of the time we have together will be to follow some specific behavioural guidelines:

> Say 'I', not 'we' or 'people', because you can never truly speak for someone else
>
> One person, one idea at a time
>
> Ask others to clarify their thinking rather than exclusively advocating your own views
>
> Look to build on what other people say rather than queuing to speak
>
> Do more listening than talking
>
> Reflect on how you have contributed to whatever problem is being discussed
>
> Consider the possibility that you don't know the 'truth' about anything; don't 'grandstand' or make speeches; follow everything you say with the phrase 'in my opinion'
>
> Be fully present: set aside the preoccupations you brought here and put away your electronic devices
>
> Speak up if you feel your time is not being used productively.

Discussing how and why these suggestions might make a difference is normally the first part of any workshop that I run with a team and gives me a degree of permission to offer the group feedback if and when they breach these 'rules'.

Summary

Jungian instruments such as the MBTI can add considerable value to team coaching or other similar processes where you are working with a group. Teams can often be dysfunctional and have deep-rooted problems whose origins lie months or years in the past. The explicitly positive focus of Jungian instruments can help to create a safe environment where it is possible to explore damaging conflicts that have been hidden up to that point. Team coaching will normally start with a careful contracting conversation followed by separately interviewing every individual in the team, before assessing where and how any psychometric instrument might find a place in the team coaching programme. Good practice also includes reassuring people about the purpose of the instrument and how results will be shared and stored, as well as allowing enough time in any workshop to explore it fully. The expert team coach works from coaching principles, understanding that the team must find its own solutions and that the role is to create the climate where this can happen.

Note

1   My book *Facilitating Groups* (Rogers 2010) has more on all of this.

12 Designing an introductory workshop

This chapter contains a selection of reliable exercises for use with groups where your aim is to introduce the MBTI or another similar Jungian psychometric questionnaire. There are hundreds of such activities, though most are variants on the same ideas and there is limited space here to include more than the ones that I find that I use again and again. CPP/OPP publish and distribute comprehensive resource guides with detailed explanations on how to use tried and tested exercises, but there are many more available free on the internet. If you enter *MBTI exercises* or *MBTI games* into your browser this will bring up websites with constantly updated suggestions and ideas. Most publishers also maintain a resources section where people they have trained and licensed can get free access to suggested exercises. The activities I describe here are based on the MBTI, but many of them will work with other Jungian instruments with little or no adaptation.

An introductory workshop: overview

Suitable for: part of a team coaching process; management development; a group where relationships matter and might need to be improved; a training course for coaches, managers, teachers, trainers or other professionals where understanding others is vital.

Many of the exercises I describe in this chapter will also work well in mediation, couple counselling and pair coaching.

Purpose: to introduce the underpinning Jungian ideas; give people the chance to experience Type in action; get clarity about their own preferences.

This is a brief outline of a format for an introductory workshop. There is detailed information on how to run exercises around each topic later in the chapter, and you will want to experiment with whatever you judge will work best for the particular group that has commissioned you.

Time: 3.5 hours.

Resources: a PowerPoint presentation, laptop, projector; flip charts, pens; a room large enough to accommodate breakout groups without too much contamination from noise. Depending on the size of the group, choose an open circle with no tables or a cabaret style layout. Both these will allow people to move about freely.

Preparation: a blank Type table on the flip chart, a PowerPoint presentation.

Assumptions: The group has already taken the questionnaire and received or scored their results, but no one has had individual feedback. Most of the time in the workshop will be spent on exercises that will enable people to review and understand their Type preferences, and there will be a minimum of talking from you. If people want more of the theory, refer them to one of the booklets or the many websites which will give more information on research and other topics.

Running order

1 A brief introduction from you which describes the origins of the questionnaire and its developers, explains what it does and does not measure and where it fits with and differs from other instruments
2 An exercise to explore the meaning of *preference*
3 You show a slide which lays out the four dimensions/Dichotomies with very brief explanations of each. You ask people to guess where they would put themselves on each, i.e. how clear or unclear they are about each preference, saying that the workshop will give them ample time to consider what is 'true' for them as they know themselves best
4 An exercise in groups to explore Extraversion/Introversion
5 An exercise in groups to explore Sensing/Intuition
6 An exercise in groups to explore Thinking/Feeling
7 An exercise in groups to explore Judging/Perceiving
8 Whole group: invite the group to look again at their results on the questionnaire. How do their guesses compare with how they actually scored?
9 Solo activity: invite people to read their Type profile. Where does it seem accurate, where inaccurate? Depending on the amount of time you have available, you might invite people to pair up to discuss this. Emphasize that you will be available during breaks to discuss any particular issues that people have with their likely profile
10 Invite people to write their names in the appropriate Type cell on the flip chart. Where people are still uncertain or unclear, ask whether they would prefer to hold off from doing this for the moment
11 Whole group: an activity to explore the Type table for this team. Which preferences or Types dominate? What balance is there between E and I, S and N, T and F, J and P?

12 A Function-alike, Quadrant-alike or Temperament-alike activity to begin the process of looking at, for example, relationship patterns, conflict, influencing and attitudes to change

13 Whole group: questions, review of learning and next steps.

Understanding the concept of preference in Jungian Type indicators: the handedness exercise

Suitable for: the first activity on an introductory workshop; working one to one with a coaching client.

Purpose: to bring the idea of preference to life; to emphasize that all of us use all eight of the preferences every day but that most of us have a natural preference, anywhere from slight or strong for one in each pair.

Time: 5–10 minutes.

Preparation: flip chart divided into two columns.

Running the exercise

1 Ask everyone to write their names and the place where they were born

2 Ask them to switch their pen to their non-dominant hand and do the same

3 Ask what the difference was

4 Chart the words people use under the headings *Preferred, Non-preferred*

5 Discuss how this applies to psychological preference.

Typical responses

For the preferred hand, the chart may include comments such as: *easy, fluent, didn't have to think, confident.* For the non-preferred hand: *felt childlike, awkward; did it but it felt clumsy; took time and concentration; not enjoyable.*

Extraversion–Introversion exercises

Purpose: to explore communication styles; to clarify, expose and explore ideas and sometimes mutual prejudice about one's own and others' preferences; to see preference-influenced behaviour in action.

Time: typically 5–10 minutes for each exercise plus debrief.

For each of the following discussion-based exercises, brief an observer to look at: the level of noise and activity, whether everyone speaks, who is silent, whether people speak over each other, how much laughter there is, whether they get to a conclusion or not.

'Upsides and downsides' exercises

1   Divide the group into E and I preferences and ask them to work at different ends of the room or in different rooms
2   Ask them to discuss any *one* of the following:

> What three questions would you like to ask the opposite preference group about their preference?
> What are the upsides of your own preference, what are the downsides?
> What do you think the [opposite] preference group feel and think about you? How would you like them to see you?
> What would it be like if organizations were composed entirely of Es or entirely of Is?

The ideal conference

Divide people into separate groups of Es and Is as before and with an observer as before. Set the following task: *Produce a single flip chart page which represents an ideal conference in your professional area. Present it any way you like.*

Typical responses

The E-preference group will often produce a crowded picture full of people and with much emphasis on discussion, breakout groups and socializing in the evenings and breaks. Some groups may not write anything, but will present their conclusions as a mini-play or sketch.

The I-preference group is more likely to produce a sparser set of images or words showing people listening intently to a presentation, sitting alone, reading, talking in pairs, taking solitary walks in beautiful scenery; when presenting, they are far more likely to have relied upon writing up their conclusions on a flip chart.

The talking-token exercise

Unlike most other E/I exercises, this one blends people of both preferences in groups of 5–7 people. Its aim is to raise awareness of patterns in contribution where people of both preferences are present – that is, most groups – and of self-awareness, for instance the urge to speak sparingly for Introverts and to speak more frequently and at greater length and at higher volume for Extraverts.

Time: 6–7 minutes plus discussion.

Resources: identical sets of coins or Lego pieces, six for each person in each group.

1 Task: to discuss the topic of *How E–I differences show themselves in organization life*.
2 Each time you speak you must lay down one of your 'talking tokens' (the coins or Lego pieces). After you have used all your tokens you cannot speak.
3 The activity is strictly timed to 5 minutes (use the timer on your phone).

Variant: no timer; the activity does not end until everyone has used all of their pieces.

Typical responses

Since the purpose of the activity is totally transparent, the talking may apparently be more evenly spread than you might expect. However, brief the observer to note not just who talks and in what order, but also how long each contribution has tended to be.

Bring the groups together again and discuss how it felt, knowing that people's usual behaviour was under scrutiny. For instance, did the E-preference people consciously moderate how and when they spoke? How much extra effort did the I-preference people have to make to take part?

Typical outcomes and responses from any E/I exercise

The observers' roles are vital. The activity usually reveals considerable differences in how the groups set about their task. The E-group's observer will usually notice high levels of cheerful noise and sometimes competitive speaking as people tumble over each other's sentences or talk at once. Most members of the group will probably contribute. By contrast, the I-group's observer will describe a quieter, more thoughtful discussion where some members may remain silent and there are longer pauses between individual contributions.

Running the discussion

- Ask the observers for their comments
- Ask the groups for their own comments
- When the groups present the output from the exercises, look out for words which convey casually harsh judgements about people of the opposite preference. For instance, an I-group will often have as one of their questions to the other group 'Are you really as boastful as you

seem?' or 'Why do you rush to fill any silence?'; and the E-group will often have questions such as 'Why do you hold back in meetings?' or 'Why won't you tell us what you're thinking?'

- Facilitate a discussion about the mutual prejudice that lies behind such statements and about the upsides and downsides of each preference
- Discuss the likelihood that there is a social bias towards Extraversion in many national cultures; if you are working with a multi-cultural or multi-national group ask them for comments on their culture of origin and how far this bias applies there
- Ask what people feel the developmental benefit might be of growing more skill in their use of the opposite preference
- Ask how well individuals feel they manage the downsides of their preference
- Ask for examples of how E/I preferences play out in meetings that group members attend
- Where you are working with a team, ask how these preferences fit with patterns of interaction in their meetings. Here, people whose preference is Introversion will often describe finding it difficult to contribute, so powerful questions to explore will be:

What might make it easier for people to contribute more evenly?
What role could meetings' leaders/chairs play?
How might the E-preference people need to moderate their behaviour?
What extra effort might the I-preference people need to make?

Sensing and Intuition exercises

Purpose: to explore in more depth what each preference means in practice and to understand their complementarity as thinking styles; to see preference-influenced behaviour in action.

A group task

Time: 7–10 minutes plus debrief.

Divide groups into S-preference and N-preference people, ideally no more than seven in each group. Form extra groups if one group seems too large.

Resources: two exactly matching packs of Lego containing a range of shapes and colours.

1 The brief is: 'make a structure' make sure you deliver it exactly like that, just three words, no further explanation. Set a timer for 5 minutes.

2   Brief the observers to look out for: what assumptions the group seems to be making about their task; how they discuss it and for how long; the language they use; how they allocate roles; what the finished structure looks like; how quickly they work.

Typical responses

The Sensing-preference group will usually set about their task with formidable concentration and ease. Often there is little discussion: the group quickly decides to create a 'bridge' or a 'tower' – something recognizably realistic. The shape is solid, the colours are expertly matched, whatever is created is usually stable, symmetrical and unornamented. The group will assume that all pieces have to be used, even though this was not part of the instruction.

The Intuitive-preference group will often start with a period of discussion or argument. They will typically work in parallel, not as a group, at least at first. The colours may be randomly used and some pieces discarded. Sometimes, even in a short exercise like this, one member of the group may become bored and sit back or walk off. The resulting 'structure' may wobble and fall apart, if it is finished at all. Occasionally group members will work entirely alone, each producing their own 'structure'.

Running the discussion

- Ask the observers to describe what they saw
- Ask each group to review the other group's 'structure'
- Explore how the Intuitive-preference group felt about working with their colleagues. Often they will describe frustration at not being able to insist on their own ideas being followed, especially if the groups contain a number of Intuitive–Thinking–Judging Types
- Ask the Sensing-preference group the same question
- Invite comment on how these preferences play out in everyday life, especially if you are working with an intact team, where, for effective problem-solving, both S and N preferences need to be honoured
- Explore the links with professions which need the skills associated with S and N, for instance that surgical or civil engineering careers often attract people with a Sensing preference because such jobs need high levels of meticulousness and willingness to follow tried and tested protocols. Careers in the Arts tend to attract people with an N preference because such careers encourage innovation and individuality.

Solo exercises

These exercises all work on the same principle. They ask people to write a short paragraph describing a topic. The aim is to demonstrate that attention typically focuses in different ways for each preference.

Preparation: Prepare a slide or a flip chart which briefly lists the ways that the theory predicts that people of the different preferences will respond to this exercise. Conceal this from the group at this stage. It could look like this:

Sensing	Intuition
Lists	Big picture
Detail, data, facts	Metaphor and simile
Physical description	Humour, whimsy
Practical	Future focus
Tangible	Imagined scenarios
Step by step	Lack of detail

There are many variants of this activity, all of which begin with the instruction to 'Write a paragraph on ...'. Here are some of the most popular:

How you got to the venue this morning
A garden
This room
A tree
A picture (either in the room or one that you have brought with you).

Running the discussion

- Show the group your slide or flip chart
- Ask for individuals who feel that what they have written is a good fit with what the theory predicts, then invite them to read their paragraph, following an Intuitive contribution with one from a Sensing-preference person
- Discuss how each preference contributes something different to problem-solving
- Explore the downsides of each preference; ask how individuals feel they manage the downsides
- Invite people whose paragraphs do *not* fit the theory to read them. This is a way of acknowledging that theory is one thing, 'reality' is another and that we all vary in how we use our preferences
- Discuss the topics of relevance to problem-solving, group life and career choice as above.

Variant: set the discussion up as a 'fishbowl', that is, with an inner circle consisting of Sensing- then Intuitive-preference people surrounded by the people of the opposite preference. You facilitate the discussion along the lines above.

Thinking and Feeling exercises

Purpose: to explore the trickiest of the four dimensions/Dichotomies and one where the names of the preferences are even more a potential source of confusion than with the other three Dichotomies, for instance that 'Feeling' does not mean sentimentality and that these preferences can be influenced by social norms and by gender. More than the other three sets of preferences, this Dichotomy may create irritation and resistance. Type Indicators that allow for nuance here are helpful – for instance, Step II of the MBTI where, depending on the instrument, you might report as a 'sensitive T' or as a 'questioning F' or somewhere in the middle. The purpose of T/F activities is to understand more about how this approach to decision-making can play out in practice. It can be a shock to T-preference participants to discover how ruthlessly they apply logic and rationality, and equally a shock to F-preference people to realize how they equivocate over making a decision that seems to be punitive in any way, even when the situation appears to call for swift action and toughness.

The activities can take two forms, both equally useful, depending on your group:

> *Case studies* are exercises in decision-making, parts of which have been written to appeal equally to Ts and Fs. What typically happens is that in the deliberately limited time available, an F-preference group only pays attention to the words and ideas that concern relationships and personal values, while the T-preference group only pays attention to the words and ideas that involve objective logic and fairness
>
> *Discussion exercises* where participants are invited to debate topics where Ts and Fs may place a radically different emphasis.

Observers play a vital role. Brief them to look out for all of the following: the language that people use; how the group behaves towards each other; how quickly they reach a conclusion; how much and what kind of emotion or energy they display in making their points.

A sample case study

I have used this case study with many hundreds of people and it works well. Feel free to use it yourself as it is or to adapt it to the sector and roles familiar to your participants.

1   Divide the group into Ts and Fs
2   Give them each a hard copy of the case study and tell them that their instructions are included in what they will read.

Time: 15 minutes plus debrief.

The case of Chris: an exercise in decision-making

You run a team of six senior people in a [name of sector] organization. Your team provides services to the rest of the organization. The business unit for which you work is now under a lot of pressure as you are having to compete with external providers of services. You have specific income targets for the coming year, and these are widely regarded as being tough to meet.

Chris is one of your team. He has worked for the organization for 33 years and is now approaching his 55th birthday. You and he have known each other for many years, in fact when you were new to the organization he was tremendously generous and helpful in passing on his knowledge to you and making you feel welcome. When your marriage was in difficulty he was the one person at work to whom you felt you could talk freely and he listened carefully and sympathetically.

Now you are his boss. The difficulty is that there have been innumerable complaints about Chris's behaviour. These concern accusations of rudeness to senior people in other departments and allegations of 'bullying' from his staff. Over the last year it has become clear that Chris is deeply unhappy with the way he sees the organization going. He says he hates the way there is so much emphasis on saving money and compromising quality and that the personal touch of the early years of the organization has been lost. He says that 'the accountants' seem to have taken over.

The organization has had a tough time in the last few years. There have been innumerable restructurings, regulators have been critical and there has been some adverse press publicity, much of it from your local media. A recent survey shows that staff engagement levels are much lower than they should be. This same survey has revealed that in Chris's own department their results are on the 20th percentile. When you have tackled him about it, he says he is simply trying to maintain the old values and standards, and that there are an awful lot of 'ignorant young people' around who don't understand the importance of tradition in what they are doing.

You are under pressure from your own boss to 'sort this – and quick!'

You know from your informal conversations with Chris that there is considerable stress in his life. His wife has suffered on and off for some years from a serious psychiatric illness and has frequent long stays in hospital. She is an inpatient at a local mental health unit at the moment. Their young teenage son has Type 1 diabetes, and Chris tells you that this is not currently well managed as the boy is not compliant with his medication and has had several recent hospital admissions as an emergency.

You have a meeting scheduled with Chris. What do you plan to do?

Typical responses

Thinking-preference groups emphasize surfacing the conflict and confronting it; where there is a performance issue, the needs of the organization must come before the needs of an individual; all-round fairness is also important, so how managers carry out these difficult conversations really matters. It would be rare for a group to propose any intermediate solution such as counselling or a referral to HR. They typically decide quickly and easily and there is often briskness to the way they discuss it. They will use words such as: *fairness, performance, review, justice, objectivity, balance, impartiality.*

Feeling-preference groups look for a harmonious solution which recognizes that the whole person is involved and that how managers deal with this kind of issue gives important messages to the rest of the organization; personal values matter and must not be betrayed. They look for a solution where the manager can feel comfortable as well as the employee, often suggesting an initial low-key meeting where the problem is explored, and counselling as a next resort; compassion is a key value; 'tough love' is often necessary in this kind of case – they agree that it may be more humane ultimately to find a way for Chris to leave the organization. The words they use will include: *kindness, warmth, friendship, empathy, rapport.* The discussion will often be slower and more thoughtful. They may not reach a final decision.

Running the discussion

- Ask each group to report their conclusions
- Ask the observers to report on what they saw and heard
- Invite each group to comment on the other group's decisions and on what they notice about how each presentation has been made
- Encourage a discussion about the value of honouring personal relationships versus the value of acting for the sake of the organization's

needs; where does compassion come before toughness, mercy before justice?

- Discuss the gender dimension: how does socialization affect this preference, for instance that women tend to be socialized towards nurturing and men towards toughness? What is it like to be a male F and a female T?
- Where there are data on how this preference is represented in the wider organization, ask how this may affect issues such as staff engagement, emphasis on results and performance management
- Discuss the dominance of T-preference senior managers in most organizations and ask why the groups think this is and what the consequences are
- Where you are working with an intact team, invite them to consider how far each preference is taken into account in their day-to-day decision-making. (Often there is an imbalance, depending on the Type preferences of the team and its leader.)

Thinking/Feeling discussion exercises

These tend to fall into two categories: a *briefer version of the case study approach*, for instance a scenario where resources are limited and a decision must be made that is bound to disadvantage someone, and a *discussion about a principle or concept*. In either case, divide the group into Thinking-preference and Feeling-preference participants.

Examples of case study exercises are:

> Your company has said it will reward one member of your team with a trip to some pleasant city for a weekend break, but you have to make the decision yourselves about what criteria you will use.
>
> Space has been reorganized in your office and two people have to hot-desk rather than having their own workspace. How will you decide who they are to be?

Examples of discussion exercises are:

> What is the best way to give people feedback?
>
> For what do you want to be appreciated at work? What happens if you do not get the recognition you need?
>
> What is love?
>
> What makes for good teamwork?

Time: 10 minutes plus debrief.

Typical responses

Thinking Types will emphasize the importance of fairness, achievement, tangible outcomes, judiciously offered feedback from someone they respect, not taking anything too personally, anger as an initial response to their apparent failure to impress and then cool disengagement and shrugging their shoulders if they experience lack of recognition.

Feeling Types will emphasize the importance of rapport, personal connection, harmony, being liked, gentleness, being recognized for helping others and for who you are as much as for what you do, authentic praise and getting upset and being demotivated by criticism because it feels so personal.

Running the discussion

Follow the steps above.

Judging and Perceiving exercises

Purpose: the Judging and Perceiving preferences are essentially about psychological differences in attitudes to time, planning and decision-making. The Judging-preference person feels relief when the decision has been made, the Perceiving-preference person wants to keep their options open for as long as possible. Behaviour around time and planning may be different for people of each preference, though beware of assuming that Js are always 'organized' while Ps are 'sloppy'. These exercises aim to help clarify which feels more comfortable for individuals and to understand the complementary value of each.

A whole-group exercise: work and play

I first met this exercise on the OPP MBTI qualifying workshop and have used it many times since. It does not usually result in neat correlations between a reported preference for J or P, but I like it all the more for that as the value is in the discussion.

Time: 15 minutes including discussion.

1 Reveal a flip chart or slide with two statements on it:

   I can play when I've finished my work
   I can play at any time

2 Ask the group to stand up and to clear away tables and chairs so that there is enough space to spread out in a line across the room

3 Say that there is now an invisible straight line across the room and that the far ends of the line represent each of the two statements and point to which is which

4 Point to where the midpoint lies

5 Ask the group to place themselves along the line according to how far they agree with either statement, so if they enthusiastically endorse the statement 'I can play at any time' they should place themselves at the very end on that side.

Typical responses and debrief discussion

- There is usually a cluster of people in the middle, but start with the outliers, the people very clear about their agreement with either statement. Ask them to say why they placed themselves where they did, then take someone from the other end of the spectrum
- Invite contributions from anyone else who wants to speak, including the people who hover at the midpoint, asking them what the pull is to either side and how they reconcile the differences
- Ask people to raise their hands if they scored for J and then do the same for those who reported as having a preference for P, though do not expect a perfect correlation, as this is rare
- When people are seated again ask them how these preferences play out in their own team's or group's decision-making style and attitudes to planning.

Discussion exercises for Judging and Perceiving

These all involve the same idea: choosing a topic on which J- and P-preference people are likely to have different behavioural patterns.

Time: 6 minutes plus debrief.

1 Divide people into J- and P-preference groups

2 Brief an observer to look for the energy and language that each group uses and at how far they actually follow the brief

3 The task: *Choose any ONE of the following for the group to discuss*:

How you prepare for a holiday/vacation
If we were to look in the boot/trunk of your car right now, what would we find?
Deadlines
Time
Plans and planning (*Variant*: What's the case for planning?)

What would it be like if teams consisted entirely of people of just Js or just Ps?

Typical responses

The J-preference group is likely to have a crisp, focused discussion, often rather serious. Their holiday preparation will usually include booking transport well in advance, buying guidebooks, booking taxis and restaurants, sometimes scheduling each day in detail. Their discussion will often describe the relief they feel at having got everything 'organized'. They like to be early, they like plans and planning and cannot conceive of a world without them. They like lists. They are highly conscious that time is limited. The car boot/trunk exercise will usually reveal that the boots/trunks of their cars are clean and empty but for first-aid and tool kits.

The P-preference group may find the whole task ludicrous or boring and decide to do something else entirely. They may tell anti-planning jokes. Their presentation may consist of a few words followed by an explosion of laughter. Their discussion, if they had it, will express their horror of being pinned down. 'Time' is a vague concept that can be stretched or fought off. Sometimes they will express intense dislike of words such as 'plan', 'deliverables' and 'objectives'. The car boot/trunk exercise rarely results in a P-preference person describing an empty compartment in any car that they own or drive exclusively. Often they will cheerfully acknowledge that it contains a vast array of objects, all there 'just in case' or because 'there's no point in tidying it up – waste of effort'.

Running the discussion

- Ask the observers to describe what they saw and heard
- Invite the groups to make their own comments on their discussions
- Discuss the disadvantages of overusing each preference
- Introduce the topic of the dominance of J-preference managers in most organizations, what might explain it and what the results are, pluses and minuses
- Ask for examples of how both Js and Ps can procrastinate and what form this takes or what the triggers are
- Ask for examples of whether people of each preference do the same behaviour in their leisure time as they do at work (Js may say they are less decisive at home, and Ps are more likely to say that they are the same)
- J- and P-preference people can drive each other crazy: do they do so in this group?
- Discuss how these preferences are complementary and the value they each add.

A Function-alike exercise

Purpose: to explore Type preferences in more depth; to identify profound differences in assumption about how organizations and individuals regard motivation, recognition and reward; to pave the way for insights into conflict-management and influencing.

Time: 10 minutes plus debrief.

I aim to use this activity during any workshop on the MBTI because it produces such infinitely rich results.

Variant: you can do a similar exercise but basing it on Temperament Types (SJ, SP, NF, NT) or Quadrant-alike Types (IN, EN, IS, ES), with material on the slide or flip chart varied accordingly.

Preparation: flip charts, a handout or set of slides. One describes the task, one has your predictions about how people of different Function preferences tend to describe what they need from organization life. Conceal this from the group until they have completed their discussions. Design several slides or flip chart pages to represent these ideas:

1   The task: divide people into Function-alike Types (ST, SF, NF, NT). Say to them that their task is: *Design your ideal organization*
2   Show them the prepared flip chart or slide describing their task

> *Design your ideal organization: time 10 minutes*
>
> What business would it be in?
> What would people be rewarded for?
> How would they be rewarded?
> What would people be disciplined for?
> What structure would the organization have?
> The culture: what would it be like to work there?

3   Bring the whole group together again. Display your pre-prepared slides or flip charts (see opposite) with your predictions of the kinds of ideas that groups usually present
4   Ask each group to present a summary of their discussion, starting with the NT group, then the ST group, then the SF group and finally the NF group
5   Pause for discussion and comment after each presentation
6   Invite the whole group to consider how far each presentation has conformed to the suggestions on your slide.

Sensing-Thinking Types (ST)	Sensing-Feeling Types (SF)	Intuitive-Feeling Types (NF)	Intuitive-Thinking Types (NT)
value:	value:	value:	value:
• Efficiency • Cost-consciousness • Monitoring through data • Honouring tradition • Punctuality • Loyalty • Taking work seriously • Tangible reward: money, titles • Clarity about roles and processes • Hierarchy • Practicality in the here and now	• Practical help for people • Being down to earth • Steady improvement, no unpleasant surprises • Realism and experience • Care for individuals • Equal shares • Rewarding through praise and status • Rewarding long service • Using tested methods • Kindness	• Work that has social value • Creativity with fun • Team work • Innovation • Harmony • Authenticity • Diversity • Being driven by strongly held values • Reward through personal praise • Respect for individuals • Emotional intelligence	• Individual competence • Flat hierarchy • Autonomy • Creativity • Only as good as your last project • Complex problem-solving • No rules except the ones we set • Reward with bigger projects • Long-term growth • Debate about ideas

Typical responses

Usually there is a high degree of correlation between what the groups produce and the suggested ideas on the slide or flip chart. This has the hidden benefit of impressing people who have expressed scepticism about whichever instrument you are using.

There is often mutual amazement at what each group produces and some blurted-out critical comment, such as 'Are you serious that you would actually like working in an organization like that?' For instance, an NT group may say they are appalled at the idea of working in what they may see as the rigidity and resistance to change that they sense in the ideal organization that their ST colleagues describe. The ST group may sneer at what they see as 'the peace and love agenda' of the NF group or the 'anarchy' that they believe they glimpse in how the NT group describe their ideal work environment. If this happens you will need to facilitate the discussion with care, reminding the group that a healthy team or organization can blend all four styles and needs and that an organization in which one psychological Type dominates might be heading for trouble in the longer term.

Running the discussion

- Invite comment on which of the four styles dominates in the group's own organization. Where the MBTI is well embedded in an organization, the profiles of the senior team may be known and public. If so, draw on this
- Ask which Function dominates in this team and what the results of such dominance are
- Ask 'What needs to happen to create more diversity in this team's/ organization's thinking and behaviour?'

Summary

Using a range of exercises with a team or group creates a live experiment in which people can come to their own conclusions about their own and other people's Types. This is a lot more memorable than simply reading a profile in a book and gives ample opportunities for team members to understand that their own ways of looking at the world are likely to be radically and productively different from those of their colleagues.

13 The team looks at itself

In working with a team, I recommend running an introductory workshop first, as described in the previous chapters, followed by one or more of the activities in this chapter. All of the exercises in the previous chapters can be shaped to elicit responses that are unique to that team or group, but here I explain a range of activities that can add extra value. See them as a menu of options that you can shape to meet the needs of the particular team you are working with.

The value of looking at other teams and their Type tables

It is easy to forget your own expertise in working with Jungian indicators. Patterns that are instantly obvious to you may not be anything like so obvious to people who are new to the whole topic. So before asking my client team to look in detail at their own Type table, I will normally spend a little time giving the group some anonymized samples of Type tables from other teams and setting them a group discussion task. This helps fine-tune people's skills and focuses attention. Create your examples from other teams that you know well where you will be able to add some background data, being careful to protect confidentiality.

It still surprises and impresses me how often the team with whom I am working will produce spookily accurate guesses and insights into what was actually going on in a group that they don't know and where they have such extremely limited data, essentially just a Type table and a few other scraps of information.

Other people's teams

Purpose: to help your group understand the implications of patterns in teams; to prepare them for looking more objectively at their own team.

Time: 10–20 minutes plus debrief.

Preparation:

- Some Type tables prepared as slides or flip charts, chosen to be varied and interesting

- A slide or flip chart with some or all of these questions:

> What immediately strikes you about this group's Type table?
> Which Function-alike Types (columns) have more people in them?
> Which Functions are sparsely populated?
> What is happening with regard to E/I and J/P in this team?
> Who, if anyone, is the sole representative of a Type or Function?
> What do you guess the strengths of this team might be?
> What do you guess the weaknesses of this team might be?
> What might their meetings be like?
> What interpersonal issues do you guess they might have?
> How might they strike the people who report to them?
> How might they strike their bosses?

The task: to review what you might guess about the group whose Type table you will examine, using some or all of the questions on the slide/flip chart.

1   Spend a little time reminding your group that they will know nothing about the groups whose Type tables they are going to see other than their Type preferences and whatever other limited information you give them and that they will have no way of assessing the maturity, levels of adjustment, intelligence or competence of any of the individuals in these groups. There will be no way of knowing how well or poorly any individual in the groups may be using their preferences, let alone how skilfully they can draw on the opposite preference. It will help if you suggest that the group garnishes their comments with words like 'may' or 'possibly' and 'might'.

2   There are various ways you can do this exercise:

Show the whole group one Type table and ask for comments. This is the quickest way to do it, but it may result in a few people dominating the discussion

Show the slide but break the group into smaller groups, divided randomly, with the instruction that each should look at a different area on the Type table and then report back

Divide the group into smaller groups and give each one a different Type table, printed out ready, and then report back.

3   Make sure the group has a handy reference guide, for instance a thumbnail Type table with very brief sketches of each Type (pages 4 and 5) or a book where they can quickly look up hints about what each Type might do.

4   Give your group the questions on the slide and, after discussion, ask
    them to report back.

You might like to see how far your own guesses or insights match those produced by groups to whom I have given these Type tables:

**Example 1: The executive team of a chain of urban sandwich shops
(boss's preference: INTJ)**

ISTJ	ISFJ	INFJ	INTJ *
ISTP **	ISFP	INFP	INTP
ESTP ****	ESFP	ENFP	ENTP *
ESTJ	ESFJ	ENFJ	ENTJ

Typical discussion output

A group discussing this Type table tends to notice immediately that there are
no fewer than six people with Sensing–Perceiving preferences, that is, they
have the SP Temperament where there is a liking for pragmatic, easy-going,
practical decision-making and expediency. They will often comment that such
people might be well suited to the fast-moving environment of their business,
where attention to details such as hygiene and portion control could be vital
to success and where swift reaction to competitor activity is also likely to be
essential. They speculate that it could be fun, if somewhat rowdy, working in
this team, especially where there are four ESTPs with their liking for jokes and
pranks. They wonder if maybe the INTJ boss is by contrast a rather serious
person, isolated with only one other NT in the team and that maybe these two
have a hard time getting their colleagues to consider the longer-term future.
With only one J-preference person in the team, they wonder about how decisions are made. The total absence of Feeling Types could be a concern if this
team is not well boosted by people elsewhere in the business who can remind
them of the importance of keeping the loyalty of their staff.

The reality

All of the above was largely true for the real-life team of youngish people on which this table was based. The business was rapidly expanding and in fact was at risk of over-trading. In working with them on a team coaching programme, it was striking how frequently they veered away from decision-making, often with distracting and very funny jokes. A topic would appear to have been closed off with a decision, only for someone to reopen it moments later with some apparently 'vital' second thought. The INTJ boss, the oldest person in the team, was exasperated by a lot of this, commenting to me and then openly to his team that he felt sometimes as if he was a teacher on playground duty, fruitlessly blowing his whistle and telling the boisterous children that lessons had to start again. He felt burdened by having to make so many of the decisions alone.

The team coaching

The first part of this programme was about staff engagement and leadership, and the MBTI was not introduced at this stage. Later, much of the work I did with this team was about encouraging them to look closely at their own behaviour patterns both individually and as a group, using the MBTI as our vocabulary. They were quick to learn and eager to put it all into practice.

During the time I was working with them, two people left happily to go to good jobs elsewhere and the company deliberately sought to shape the vacancy profiles in a way that would appeal respectively to E/ISTJ-preference and E/INFJ-preference people, a quest that was successful, though of course the MBTI was not used in the actual selection process. The company also appointed an HR director (ENFJ) who expertly created and implemented a policy to raise their rate of staff retention and to train shop managers in essential leadership skills. Their own view was that the MBTI gave them a quicker grasp of the necessity for all of this than could have been achieved any other way.

Example 2: The senior team in a publishing company
(boss's preferences: ESTJ)

ISTJ	ISFJ	INFJ	INTJ
*	**	*	
ISTP	ISFP	INFP	INTP
	**	*	*
ESTP	ESFP	ENFP	ENTP
		*	
ESTJ	ESFJ	ENFJ	ENTJ
*			

Typical discussion output

A group will observe that this team is heavily weighted towards people with a preference for Introversion: eight out of a team of ten. They wonder if this means that there are problems with communication. They also notice that there are seven people with a preference for Feeling while the boss is an ESTJ, and if typical of ESTJs, may like large-scale efficiency, which could bring him or her face to face with resistance if any proposed change appeared to damage individuals. The group may also wonder if this group avoids conflict because it would disturb the Feeling preference for harmony. Some groups will wonder if the boss is new and has been brought in to create a tougher commercial environment with the ISTJ as a close colleague. Where there are so many senior people with a preference for Feeling, some participants imagine that there could be problems with performance management where a pleasant, friendly surface conceals reluctance to tackle staff whose skills are no longer what the organization needs. At the same time, one frequent comment is that there is at least one representative of each Function (ST, SF, NF and NT) and an equal number of Js and Ps.

The reality

Much of this was the case with the real-life team. Their culture was one of mutual warmth and loyalty. Many of them had worked in the company since its beginnings and the majority were women. No one's birthday was ever forgotten; weddings and new babies were celebrated in style. Their quintessential problem was that consensus had got out of control as a way of making decisions. Too many staff were involved, too many staff had to be 'happy' and too often there were pleas for 'more time to do a little bit more research'. There were many costly last-minute hold-ups at the production stage because some important error had been discovered. There was no appraisal system and few people had much idea of how their bosses rated their performance. The result was books and other products that were expensive and often missed the moment when they would have made maximum impact. Turnover and profit were declining sharply.

The team coaching

The doughty ESTJ boss commissioned what she called a 'spying survey' to kick off our work, to discover, not to her surprise, that their own publishing schedules were nearly twice as long as those of competitors and a lot more complicated. The challenge of the team coaching was to preserve the best of the existing culture while introducing greater clarity around roles, along with shorter, more efficient decision-making processes and improved performance management. This was the first focus of the team coaching. Later, I introduced them to the MBTI where the heart of our work was understanding what both Thinking and Feeling had to offer in an effective organization. One turning point was learning a new way of giving straightforward feedback which neither hurt the other person nor dodged away from difficult messages.

Example 3: Senior Customer Service team in a retail organization (boss's preferences: ENTJ)

ISTJ *	ISFJ	INFJ	INTJ
ISTP	ISFP	INFP	INTP *
ESTP	ESFP	ENFP	ENTP *******
ESTJ	ESFJ	ENFJ	ENTJ *

Typical discussion output

In this ten-person team there are seven people who report as ENTP; the boss and one other person are also in the NT column. This leave only one non-NT: the person whose preferences are ISTJ. Discussion often centres around that person, wondering whether he or she is painfully isolated and feels 'different'. People also usually notice that of the ten people, eight have preferences for Extraversion which, they think, might lead to noisy team meetings and ones where decisions are rarely final when eight out of the ten prefer P. What is the impact of so many ENTPs in one group? People read the ENTP Type description and often laugh, speculating that the climate will be lively, full of innovative ideas, loud and competitive, with a lot of jousting about who might be the most competent person. If this gets out of hand, some people wonder if the climate could become toxic, though it might also be full of creativity. There is no one in this team with a preference for F. 'I bet they did a lot of T humour' said one discussion member, 'meaning what so many Ts see as "humour", that is, sarcasm disguised as wit'. When participants look at this Type table they do not know what the gender balance is, but some wonder about what it might be like if all those ENTPs were men. With only one person whose preference is Sensing, and only two with a preference for J, some groups wonder how good this team might be at practicality and planning.

The reality

This was a team in trouble. Their bosses were impatient with slipping deadlines on a newly commissioned IT system; as a group this team was finding it difficult to accept personal responsibility for failings in how shop-floor staff were trained to handle customer complaints and was inclined to put the blame elsewhere in the company. Team members complained about each other outside team meetings and their own staff made occasional allegations about bullying. However, it was not all downsides. What was going for this team was their boisterous energy, their intelligence, their willingness to learn and their typical NT commitment to competence.

The team coaching

We started this work with a structured look at their challenges, internal and external. Then the spotlight was on relationships inside the team, using the MBTI. I had already fed back to them that I noticed how often, with so many Extravert-preference people in the team, they talked over each other and that it was rare for anyone to build on another person's comment. 'Discussion' was a series of competing statements or mini speeches. They had to learn how to speak one at a time and how to listen.

Half way through the programme, the ISTJ in the team, struggling with workload and some upsetting personal issues, had gone off work with 'stress' and in fact was never to return.

We did some exacting work on their relationships where they learned to extend their influencing styles by understanding more about how the 15 other Types might want to be influenced, As one of them said at one stage, 'Now we have to be competent at relationships. We have to learn that Feeling stuff even if it feels like we're working with our left hands all the time, damn it!'

Looking at your team

Suitable for: any team or group where working together is important.

Time: 30–60 minutes, or more, depending on the time available.

1   The most straightforward way to run this activity is to give the group the same questions (above) that they considered for the Type tables of other teams. If you did not run this activity, then use the same slide with the same general introduction.

2   Invite pairs or trios to consider the first question: what immediately strikes you about your group's Type table? Let them discuss this for about 5 minutes, and then facilitate an informal discussion on the basis of what they say.

3   Keep the group together now as you work through the remaining questions, at each stage asking for links to how these patterns play out in the group's life, for instance:

With E/I patterns: how does this affect whether you use email or meet face to face? What are your meetings like? How hard is it for the Is to get heard? (Make sure you actually ask the Is to answer this question)

With S/N patterns: how do problems get solved?

With T/F patterns: which mode of decision-making dominates? How do you compensate for this to prevent lopsidedness? If there is a staff engagement survey to draw on, ask what it reveals about how staff feel they are managed

With J/P patterns: if there is a dominance of J-preference people, ask whether there might be a compulsion to make decisions too soon. If so, how might topics be kept open for longer? If there is a predominance of P-preference people, ask whether it is possible that decision-making is avoided and how it might be speeded up.

4   Where you have people who are Type or Quadrant opposites (EN, ES, IN, IS), ask how they manage their relationship. If it is going well, ask them to say how much of this is about taking time to understand each other's differences. If it is not going well, ask what might need to happen to improve it using the lens of Type.

5   Ask people to refer back to the explanatory booklets or other material you have given them. Say, 'Take a few minutes to make some notes about presenting the essence of your Type preferences to others in the team, where you think this profile fits and where it doesn't. What would you like them to know about you?' Invite each person to speak for about 3 minutes, followed by a minute of questions to each person for clarification.

6   In the final 10 minutes of this activity, ask the team to suggest or return to changes they might want to make to improve or build on any of the areas highlighted by the discussion. Note these points in order to return to them at the action-planning phase of the whole event.

Influencing others

Purpose: to explore how understanding of others' Type preferences can increase the chances of influencing them successfully.

Suitable for: improving team relationships; management development workshops; pair coaching, coach training; sales training; any training event where teaching and learning is part of the purpose.

Time: 20 minutes plus discussion.

Without the benefit of training, most of us naïvely assume that other people like to be influenced in exactly the same way as we do ourselves. By 'influencing' I mean any situation in which what you want and what the other person wants might be different. This could include giving them instructions, working with them on how to change some aspect of their behaviour, defusing a crisis or negotiating a contract. This skill is also at the core of selling, whether you are selling an idea or an actual product and whether or not your role formally involves selling.

Teams often need to raise their game in terms of how skilfully they have discussions, create alliances with stakeholders, formulate strategy – and much more. The MBTI offers a wonderful way of learning how to do this. The immediate benefit of this exercise with a team is that it makes clear how profound Type differences are when it comes to influencing. This is a high-energy and enjoyable exercise with a serious purpose.

The task: to influence someone of an opposite or radically different Type from your own, using *their* preferred modes of communication and persuasion. Your job is to *interest them in the holiday you have most enjoyed recently. (Variant: interest them in a book or article you have recently read or a film you have recently seen.)*

Set people up in pairs so that they are working with people who are actual Type opposites, or from different Quadrants or Functions.

Make sure they have some reference material – for instance, a book of Type profiles or a slide or handout you have prepared which might look something like Table 13.1, giving them 5 minutes to prepare:

1   Time each round. Ask the opposite preference partner to give feedback on how well this went for them. Was this a good example of influencing them in their style? Then swap over and repeat
2   Bring the group together again and discuss how easy or difficult it was to put yourself in the other person's Type shoes
3   Raise the question of how to use these insights in everyday negotiating with each other and with other key people in their work environment.

Typical discussion output
Mostly people report how overwhelmingly difficult it is to sustain a conversation in the opposite Type mode. 'It felt clumsy, I couldn't believe how hard it was'; 'Felt like I was talking in a foreign language'; 'We were both laughing at how tricky it was'. Participants will often comment on the sudden insight this gives into how rooted we are in our own assumptions, describing the effort it took to sustain a conversation from an opposite set of assumptions, even though the exercise is so short. Despite the difficulties, the recipient of the attempt at persuasion often describes a successful outcome: 'He did interest me in that holiday – those were exactly the things that I take into account

Table 13.1 Influencing people of different Types

Sensing-Thinking Types value:	Sensing-Feeling Types value:	Intuitive-Feeling Types value:	Intuitive-Thinking Types value:
Specifics, facts	Practicality, realism	Enthusiasm	Big-picture thinking
The here and now	Personal connection	Authenticity	Analysing, problem-solving
Practicality	Social details and courtesies	Big ideas with social value	Logic and rationality
Step-by-step approach	Step-by-step approach	Feeling connected to others	Autonomy
Logical framework	Practical benefits to people	Personal growth	Creativity, novelty
Value for money	Friendliness	Novelty, freshness	Options and possibilities
Stability, certainty	Simplicity	Team work	Productivity
Sensible goals	Straightforwardness	Co-operation	Being unique, the first
Being business-like	Tradition	Solving problems	Long-term trends
		Ideals, dreams	Ingenuity
Don't like:	**Don't like:**	**Don't like:**	**Don't like:**
Waffle and sentimentality	Personal criticism	Phoney friendliness	Too much detail too soon

when I'm choosing', or, this from an NT who was pitched a skiing holiday in Scotland from her SP partner:

> She appealed to my need for competence and individuality, telling me how it was possible even as a complete beginner to make rapid progress as a novice skier, and that the hotel was a boutique establishment that it took a person of discrimination to appreciate! Even though I hate cold and snow and I'm not very sporty, I did get interested and will consider it!

An exercise in robust problem-solving

Purpose: to increase participants' capacity to make high-quality decisions

Suitable for: team coaching; any group where decision-making is involved; creativity workshops.

Time: 60 minutes.

It would be comparatively rare to work with a team where there is an even spread of Types, Temperaments or Functions. Even where there is such a spread, in practice the team is often dominated by a few more assertive or senior individuals. The complete absence of Feeling-preference Types in senior executive teams is extremely common, potentially leading to ignoring or downplaying the human dimension of any of their decisions. All of this can lead to a pattern of decision-making which is flawed. Type theory suggests that, at an unconscious level, we go straight to our dominant Function (see page 56) when we have to solve a problem, often at the expense of the other three Functions to which we will pay little or no attention.

There are various ways you can run this activity. This is the most straightforward:

1   Show the group the diagram in Figure 13.1, saying that it represents a way to bring the strengths of each of the four Functions (Sensing, Intuition, Thinking and Feeling) to bear on any problem

2   Ask the group to nominate a real-life organizational problem that is not too complex to be discussed in the available time

3   Divide them into Dominant-preference-alike groups
    Dominant Sensing: ISTJ, ISFJ, ESFP, ESTP
    Dominant Intuition: INTJ, INFJ, ENTP, ENFP
    Dominant Thinking: INTP, ISTP, ESTJ, ENTJ
    Dominant Feeling: INFP, ISFP, ENFJ, ESFJ

4   Set up a 'fishbowl': one group in the middle, the rest listening around the outside. Ask each group in turn to look at the issue through the part of the diagram that represents their dominant preference, starting at the top left with Sensing, then moving around clockwise to

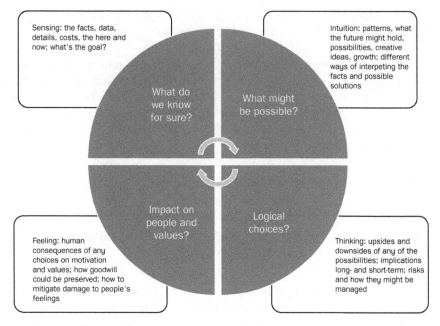

Sensing: the facts, data, details, costs, the here and now; what's the goal?

Intuition: patterns, what the future might hold, possibilities, creative ideas, growth; different ways of interpeting the facts and possible solutions

What do we know for sure?

What might be possible?

Impact on people and values?

Logical choices?

Feeling: human consequences of any choices on motivation and values; how goodwill could be preserved; how to mitigate damage to people's feelings

Thinking: upsides and downsides of any of the possibilities; implications long- and short-term; risks and how they might be managed

Figure 13.1 Using the strengths of all four Functions

Intuition then Thinking then Feeling. (If you have no one in the group with that Dominant, consider asking someone who has that preference as their Auxiliary or playing that role yourself. Alternatively, ask for volunteers who could think themselves into that preference for purposes of the exercise.) Keep each phase strictly to 5 minutes, otherwise the other preferences begin to intrude

5 Reassemble the whole group to consider the problem again. What do they now feel is the best decision? How will they take it forward? How will they mitigate the impact of any risks and downsides?

6 Ask them to compare this with the way they normally make decisions. How far do they consider each of the four Functions? What changes might they want to make in their processes and practice?

Having shown this approach to problem-solving to innumerable teams (based on the well-known MBTI 'Z-shape', see also Figure 9.1), most of them will say that they have now embedded it into the process of their discussions, regardless of which preferences dominate in that team, and that their decision-making is better rounded and more robust as a result.

Dealing with stress

Purpose: to break through the sense of invulnerability that so many individuals develop as a way of protecting themselves; to create a climate of trust and openness.

Time: 5 minutes per person plus 10 minutes of whole-group discussion.

This is a simple exercise which can be invaluable as a way of encouraging people to be honest, to open up and to talk from the heart about what stresses them. It also encourages colleagues to spot the symptoms of stress in others and to understand how to offer help. As the facilitator you need to be certain that you can create a trusting, safe environment with confidentiality absolutely assured. It is not uncommon for people to break down, maybe because of the relief at being, at last, able to talk openly about what has been hidden as too worrying to face, shameful or humiliating.

You might also like to combine this with an explanation of what Jungian thinking has to say about stress and the Inferior Function, combining this exercise with similar questions and explanations to those you might use one to one (page 79).

1   Ask each person to read the material on what tends to stress people of their Type (see Chapter 6, pp. 78–93), without conveying that all of it will apply to them (because it will not) – and that they should feel free to ignore or add to this material as they see fit. Using a pre-prepared slide or flip chart, say that you will be asking each person to describe:

What the triggers for stress are for me
How I feel when under stress
What you may see me do under stress
What helps me recover equilibrium.

2   Let each person speak uninterrupted for about 4 minutes, then ask for comments or questions before moving on to the next person
3   When each person has spoken, run a discussion on how far there are organizational pressures which could be alleviated and how pressure and stress might be better managed at team level.

An alternative exercise can be set up in the same way, with people considering the same material but under the headings of *sad*, *mad* and *glad*: 'What do I get sad about? What do I get mad about? What I am glad about?'

Summary

The personality Type exercises in this chapter are geared towards working as a team coach with a specific group and assume that you will already have done some introductory work on Type with the group. This could be individual feedback sessions or the kind of half-day workshop described in the previous two chapters. The activities in this chapter are focused on the unique characteristics of one team and the individuals in it and assume that the group is prepared to invest time in improving their ability to work with each other. The time available will limit how many of these exercises you will be able to use: pick the ones that seem most appropriate for that particular team.

Conclusion

Psychometrics have many more applications than their use in coaching. Nonetheless, there is much to be said for using them. Personality Type indicators, in particular, have much to offer because they give any coach the chance to work from a strengths-based approach with the client. They are a safe way of discussing difference and of tackling potential weaknesses.

One of their most compelling advantages is the way that indicators such as the MBTI give coach and client a common psychological vocabulary:

> Steve (ESTJ) is discussing family issues with his coach. Ruefully he says, 'I want my daughter to take piano lessons because I think it's such a fine way to introduce a love of music. She has been incredibly resistant.' Steve and his coach agree that even though his daughter is only 9 years old, it is probably already clear that her preferences are ENTP. Steve lets out a huge laugh as he suddenly realizes that the ESTJ way to persuade, which is through goals, tangible rewards and milestones, is most unlikely to work with his daughter who is more than a match for him when it comes to tactics. 'What do you need to do to persuade an ENTP?' asks his coach. 'Hmm,' says Steve, 'dangle competence in front of her, tell her she could be unique, she could compose songs to entertain her friends . . . ? OK, I get it!'

Clients can also become experts in 'Type-watching', making good guesses about the preferences of their colleagues, even when these colleagues have not taken the questionnaire – and flexing their approaches accordingly. Type concepts judiciously applied are one of the shortest of cuts to effective influencing, the number one skill that any leader or manager absolutely must have. Type concepts also have applications in leadership, career, mediation, counselling and all kinds of problem-solving, largely because they are so readily understandable and do not judge people as having too much or too little of any particular kind of behavioural trait. Where that aspect is what you need, there are many other excellent psychometric assessments which will do a good job.

When I consider my own continuing loyalty to Jungian concepts and to magnificent questionnaires such as the MBTI, I realize that one of the reasons why it has continued to fascinate me is that it mirrors one of the core values of coaching, the partnership of equals that underpins everything about how coach and client work most effectively together. It is inevitable that I bring my own INTJ preferences into everything I do with a client; these preferences are inalienably a part of who I am and I will bring my authentic self into every coaching conversation, yet I have to enter the world of the client who will have their own unique way of expressing whatever their preferences are. Every time I feel the temptation to offer the client a little box and arrow diagram or to explain a neat theory on leadership, I mentally rein myself in and ask, 'How much of this comes from my agenda? How much does this client need to know this theory?' or 'This interests me, an INTJ, but is it likely to interest or be useful to my client?' Coaching enables the client to make better choices, but this noble aim can only work if the coach is on the same self-awareness journey. Other psychometrics can do a similar job, but there is something about the unfussy neatness of the MBTI which makes it accessible, memorable and infinitely flexible.

Personality Type indicators, uniquely, are as useful with groups as they are with individuals, a method of working with teams to give them insight into their own dynamics. As with individual work, they can dismantle hostility and resistance, an effective route into the many difficulties work teams can have with defining their roles, with how they relate to each other and with how they square their need for autonomy with their need to work together. Unlike any other psychometric, Jungian indicators lend themselves to vivid, engaging exercises where people can observe Type preferences in action for themselves and come to their own conclusions:

> I remember the afternoon you introduced us to the MBTI. It was a hot July day and we had the windows open on that ground-floor room. I had always found some of my colleagues baffling, but it all suddenly made sense to me. I saw Nick, the joker of the team, abruptly vault right out of that window when he couldn't have his way with that Sensing–Intuition exercise, and solemn old Jeff, our somewhat woebegone miserabilist, offer us the essential facts that so many of the rest of us were ignoring when we did the Z-shape problem-solving exercise. Yes, Nick, INTP; Jeff, ISTJ; me, ENFP – and all the others. How could we ever have thought that a 'good' team was one where everyone thinks alike! We incorporated so many of those ideas into our routine ways of working, and everything is so very much better.

Despite hostility from rival psychometricians, Jungian concepts have endured. When I have looked at internet threads following the publication of yet another article attacking the MBTI, there is usually someone who asks, 'If it's all rubbish, why do so many people seem to believe it?' The answer of course is, firstly, that it is not 'rubbish' because it is grounded in solid research; and secondly, it is popular because it works and can be understood either at the simplest of levels or in depth and with an extraordinarily wide range of people.

Enthusiasm for Type concepts needs to be balanced by understanding their drawbacks and weaknesses. Personality Type is not a religion where faith is essential to membership of the club. It is fine to be sceptical about some aspects of the theory and to be choosy about the applications that you like as well as selecting which version of which questionnaire you endorse. This will depend on your own needs, your judgements about quality, the fit with your client group, what they can afford and your own views about what seems right for you. You will need to balance the investment in time and money that you make in getting trained with how far this is likely to pay off in your practice as well as how much it is likely to contribute to your own personal development journey.

For me, the MBTI has remained a source of inspiration, amusement and enlightenment. It has profoundly affected how I see myself and how I understand the complex world of human emotion and interaction. As Jung said about his own typology, 'It is a compass point in the wilderness of human personality', but without a compass we would certainly find everything a lot more difficult.

I am interested in your comments and questions about this book. My email address is Jenny@JennyRogersCoaching.com

Glossary

360 feedback A process which involves collected comments from a range of sources around a manager. Can be done by internet-delivered questionnaire or through structured interviews as the basis of a narrative report

Bias Questionnaire development should assess its proof against bias, that is, when one group of users finds it harder to cope with the instrument than others, suggesting that age, nationality, race or gender could be the cause

Big Five or Five Factor model This is the popular way of referring to a statistically based analysis of five overarching factors in human personality. The factors are Openness, Conscientiousness, Extraversion, Agreeableness and Neuroticism

Dichotomies In Jungian thinking, this describes the four dimensions or poles of opposites in personality: Extraversion v Introversion, Sensing v Intuition, Thinking v Feeling, Judging v Perceiving

Emotional intelligence (EQ) Concept popularized by Daniel Goleman identifying an alternative to IQ. Suggests that managing ourselves and rapport with others is as important as cognitive elements such as verbal reasoning

Extraversion In most Jungian instruments this means getting your energy from contact with people and from activity

Face validity One of the measures of success in any psychometric instrument: how far its users judge its results to be acceptable against what it claims to be its aims

Feeling One of the pair of decision-making preferences in Jungian questionnaires, representing a preference for relationship and value-based decision processes. The opposite of the Thinking preference

Function (Mental Function) A specific term used in Jungian psychology to describe four different cognitive ways of perceiving and deciding: Sensing and Intuition, Thinking and Feeling

Indicator Used to name psychometric questionnaires as an acknowledgment that they are not designed to be the last word on personality or on other factors such as ability

Introversion In most Jungian instruments this means getting your energy from quiet reflection

Intuition (often written as iNtution to represent N in Jungian questionnaires) Represents a way of perceiving the world through overall patterns and possibilities. The opposite of the Sensing Function

Ipsative A feature of psychometric questionnaires where items are offered on a forced-choice basis. The items are designed so that each may look equally desirable

Item The trigger or question in a psychometric instrument

Judging One of the pair of preferences/Dichotomies added by Myers and Briggs to Jung's typology. It means a preference for being planned and organized, the opposite of the Perceiving preference

Judging Function refers to the Thinking–Feeling dimension/Dichotomy which is about how we typically make decisions

Jungian questionnaires Psychometric questionnaires based on the ideas of Carl Jung (1875–1961) in his book *Psychological Types* where he identified eight ways of thinking which then influence behaviour. His ideas are the basis of the MBTI and many other questionnaires

Likert scale An alternative to ipsative items. Instead of forced choice, the user is invited to opt for a choice on a scale, e.g. 1–5, representing how far they agree with any particular statement; an 'in the middle' choice is therefore possible

Meta-analysis A systematic statistical review of several studies which may combine quantitative and qualitative data as a way of creating an overall conclusion which has more strength than any of the individual studies. This was the process used to create the Big Five psychometric approach

NLP Neuro-Linguistic Programming, an approach to behavioural change invented by Richard Bandler in the 1970s, claiming to 'reprogram' the brain according to certain assumptions or 'presuppositions'

Norm group A number of people who have taken a psychometric questionnaire or test and who are then used as a reference point. Norm groups may be random samples or may represent a particular age, profession or other cohort of people

Normal distribution The bell-shaped curve produced when a number of measurements are plotted on a graph, producing scores which cluster around the middle, the top of the curve, decreasing as the distance from the middle increases

Perceiving One of the pair of preferences/Dichotomies added by Myers and Briggs to Jung's typology. It means a preference for keeping options open and remaining adaptable; the opposite of the Judging preference

Perceiving Function This refers to the Sensing–Intuition dimension/Dichotomy about where your attention typically first goes

Preference This is used in the MBTI and other Jungian-based questionnaires to describe how far an individual prefers one of a pair of four sets of dimensions/Dichotomies (Extraversion–Introversion, Sensing–Intuition, Thinking–Feeling, Judging–Perceiving)

Psychometrics The science of measuring human personality, behaviour and ability

Reliability One of the core psychometric principles: an instrument is said to be reliable if it produces consistent results with the same or similar people over time

Raw scores The sum total of a number of answers without any sort of adjustment having been made against a norm group, e.g. the number of correct answers in a verbal reasoning test

Sensing In most Jungian instruments this means perceiving the world through what is tangible in the here and now; the opposite of the preference for Intuition

Sten scores Sten is short for *standard ten*, meaning a ten-point scale produced after raw scores have been compared with those of a norm group

Team coaching A process where a work team meets regularly with a coach to work on its roles, relationships, systems and structures. The aim is to improve performance by improving the capacity of the team to deal with its current and future challenges

Temperament Temperament Types are associated today with the work of David Keirsey (1921–2013) and strongly aligned with the MBTI. But the idea of four Temperaments has a long history, starting with Hippocrates' (460–370 BC) theory of Cheerful, Sombre, Enthusiastic and Calm types of personality. Keirsey named his version Artisan (Sensing Perceiving), Guardian (Sensing Judging), Idealist (Intuitive Feeling) and Rationalist (Intuitive Thinking)

Test–retest One of the main ways in which reliability is measured. It means administering the same test to the same people after a period of time has elapsed. A psychometric instrument is considered reliable when it produces the same result when re-administered to the same person

Thinking One of the two decision-making preferences/Dichotomies in Jungian questionnaires, representing a preference for objectivity and logic; the opposite of the Feeling preference

Trait-based instrument A psychometric questionnaire which measures how the person behaves on a number of different scales such as Openness or Determination. Trait-based instruments *measure*, whereas Type-based instruments *sort*

Type-based instrument This classifies people into personality types on the assumption that these are stable characteristics which do not vary much over a lifetime

Type development The assumption in Jungian psychology that each individual is on a unique lifelong path towards some ability to develop use of all the mental processes and Functions and that there is a typical pattern associated with different life stages

Type dynamics The MBTI endorses the belief that there is a natural hierarchy of Functions for each Type: Dominant, Auxiliary, Tertiary and Inferior, which may be Introverted or Extraverted according to a formula developed by Isabel Myers, based on aspects of Jung's thinking

Typology In psychometrics this means a particular and systematic approach to categorizing human personality

Validity Whether a questionnaire measures what it claims to measure

Bibliography and further reading

Bayne, R. (1997) *The Myers–Briggs Type Indicator: A Critical Review and Practical Guide*. Cheltenham: Stanley Thornes

Bridges, W. (2004) *Transitions: Making Sense of Life's Changes* (25th anniversary edition). Cambridge, MA: Da Capo Press

Brock, S.A. (1994) *Introduction to Type and Selling*. Mountain View, CA: CPP

Cain, S. (2013). *Quiet: The Power of Introverts in a World that Can't Stop Talking*. New York: Penguin Books

Dunning, D. (2005) *Type and Career Development*. Mountain View, CA: CPP

Goffee, R. and Jones, G. (2006) *Why Should Anyone be Led By You?* Boston, MA: Harvard Business School Publishing

Goleman, D. (1996) *Emotional Intelligence: Why It Can Matter More than IQ*. London: Bloomsbury

Ibarra, I. (2003) *Working Identity: Unconventional Strategies for Reinventing Your Career*. Boston, MA: Harvard Business School Publishing

Keirsey, D. (1998) *Please Understand Me II. Temperament, Character, Intelligence*. Del Mar, CA: Prometheus Nemesis

Kahneman, D. (2012) *Thinking, Fast and Slow*. London: Penguin Books

Krebs Hirsh, S. and Kise, J.A. (2011) *Introduction to Type and Coaching*. Mountain View, CA: Consulting Psychologists Press

Kroeger, O. and Thuesen, J.M. (1988) *Type Talk*. New York: Dell Publishing

Lencioni, P. (2002) *The Five Dysfunctions of a Team: A Leadership Fable*. San Francisco, CA: Jossey-Bass

Luft, J. and Ingham, H. (1955). *The Johari Window, a graphic model of interpersonal awareness*. Proceedings of the Western Training Laboratory in Group Development. Los Angeles, CA: University of California, Los Angeles

Myers, I.B. (1998) *Introduction to Type* (6th edn). Sunnyvale, CA: CPP

Myers, I.B., McCaulley, M.H., Quenk, N.L. and Hammer, A.L. (1998) *MBTI Manual: A Guide to the Development and Use of the Myers–Briggs Type Indicator Instrument*. Mountain View, CA: CPP

Myers, I.B. and Myers, P. (1980) *Gifts Differing: Understanding Personality Type*. Palo Alto, CA: Consulting Psychologists Press

Myers, K.D. and Kirby, L.K. (1994) *Introduction to Type Dynamics and Development*. Oxford: Oxford Psychologists Press

Palmer, H. and Brown, P. (1998) *The Enneagram Advantage*. New York: Harmony Books

Passmore, J. (ed.) (2008) *Psychometrics in Coaching*. London: Kogan Page

Pearman, R., Lombardo, M.M. and Eichinger, R.W. (2005) *YOU: Being More Effective in Your MBTI Type*. Minneapolis, MN: Lominger

Pemberton, C. (2015) *Resilience: A Practical Guide for Coaches*. Maidenhead: Open University Press

Quenk, N.L. (2002) *Was That Really Me?* Palo Alto, CA: Davies Black; Consulting Psychologists Press

Richmond, S.L. (2008) *Introduction to Type and Leadership*. Palo Alto, CA: CPP

Rogers, J. (2007a) *Influencing Others Using the Sixteen Personality Types* (2nd edn). London: Management Futures; Milton Keynes: ASK Europe

Rogers, J. (2007b) *Sixteen Personality Types at Work in Organisations* (2nd edn). London: Management Futures; Milton Keynes: ASK Europe

Rogers, J. (2010) *Facilitating Groups*. Maidenhead: Open University Press

Rogers, J. (2011) *Job Interview Success: Be Your Own Coach*. Maidenhead: Open University Press

Rogers, J. (2016) *Coaching Skills: The Definitive Guide to Being a Coach* (4th edn). Maidenhead: Open University Press

Saunders, F.W. (1991) *Mother's Light, Daughter's Journey*. Palo Alto, CA: CPP

Schein, E. (2006) *Career Anchors: Self Assessment* (3rd edn). New York: Pfeiffer

Schutz, W. (1989) *Profound Simplicity*. San Diego, CA: WSA Bantam

Stevens, A. (1994) *Jung: A Very Short Introduction*. Oxford: Oxford University Press

Waterman, J. and Rogers, J. (1997) *Introduction to the FIRO-B Instrument*. Mountain View, CA: Consulting Psychologists Press

Waterman, J. and Rogers, J. (2010) *Introduction to the FIRO Business Instrument*. Mountain View, CA: CPP

Watts, G. and Morgan, K. (2015) *The Coach's Casebook*. Cheltenham: Inspect & Adapt

Yalom, I. (2002) *The Gift of Therapy*. London: Judy Piatkus

Resources

The original MBTI materials in their various formats, the Strong Interest Inventory, the FIRO-B questionnaire, the 16PF and the Thomas–Kilmann Conflict Mode Instrument (TKI) are available from OPP in the UK. OPP runs a comprehensive training programme backed up by an extensive range of further workshops. Contact www.opp.com

CPP-published books and materials listed above are generally available from OPP in the UK, or contact www.cpp.com in the US

CAPT.org (Center for Applications of Psychological Type) trains and licenses people in MBTI assessments in the US and is also the main repository of research into the MBTI. www.capt.org

For other Jungian instruments, see Chapter 3.

Resources available from www.JennyRogersCoaching.com

Free: a quick version of a Jungian Type questionnaire.

Sixteen Personality Types at Work in Organisations, 2nd edition (Rogers 2007b).

This 36-page book is designed to be used with groups or with individuals. The book devotes an easily read page to each personality Type. The focus is on work: preferred style of boss, of working, leadership style. It has a simple but comprehensive description of MBTI theory plus constantly updated data on Type frequency and distribution based on a large sample of British managers.

Influencing Others Using the Sixteen Personality Types (Rogers 2007a). This is the companion book to the above. It explores how to make practical use of each personality Type in handling conflict, persuasion and influencing, first by understanding how your own Type affects your preferred ways of influencing and being influenced, secondly by understanding that other Types need different approaches. Useful for team coaching and also in couple counselling as well as with individual coaching clients.

Index

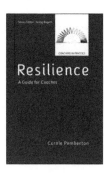

Resilience
A practical guide for coaches

Carole Pemberton

ISBN: 978-0-335-26374-5 (Paperback)
eBook: 978-0-335-26375-2
2015

Resilience: A Guide for Coaches is based on the author's experience as an expert executive and career coach. Inspired by her own research with individuals who have lost their resilience; it provides key insights from psychology, case study evidence and tools for coaches to work with on resilience issues.

Practicing or training coaches can gain:

- An understanding of what resilience is, and what separates it from burnout and trauma
- A range of approaches that they can use in working with resilience issues
- A better understanding of the their own resilience

www.mheducation.co.uk

Manager as Coach
The new way to get results

Rogers, Whittleworth and Gilbert

ISBN: 9780077140182 (Paperback)
eBook: 9780077140199
2012

How do you manage performance?

If you come across as too directive you may get a reputation for harshness. If you are too nice you risk being known as gullible and easily outmanoeuvred. Neither approach works.

'Employee engagement' is the magical ingredient: it makes staff genuinely committed, creating excellent work. Few organizations actually achieve it, though all say they want it. Coaching is the most reliable way of producing it.

Manager as Coach challenges many of the traditional assumptions about what works in management and shows you, step by step, how to be a brilliant manager and get fantastic results:

    Reduce your stress
    Develop employees' key skills
    Create a culture of engagement
    Improve bottom line results

www.mheducation.co.uk

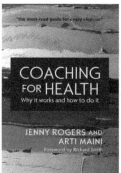

Coaching for Health
Why it Works and How to do it

Jenny Rogers and Arti Maini

ISBN: 978-0-335-26230-4 (Paperback)
eBook: 978-0-335-26231-1
2016

This book has a radical new message for any clinician: through coaching you reduce your own stress and you get far better outcomes for patients. 'Coaching for health' means creating a different relationship in consultations, asking a different kind of question and giving information in a different way. It goes beyond what is usually meant by 'patient-centred practice'. It will work with virtually any patient. When you take a coaching approach the chances are that your patients gain confidence in managing their own health, reduce the number of appointments they request, are less likely to need emergency admissions and are more likely to take their medication.

Coaching is not just a technique that you switch on and off, it is a wholly different mindset. Coaching for Health explains the rationale for a coaching approach and gives pragmatic step by step help on how to do it.

The authors - one an executive coach, one a doctor - write from their extensive, collective experience. Having trained many hundreds of clinicians in coaching skills, Jenny Rogers and Arti Maini have seen firsthand how transforming it can be to use in practice.

www.mheducation.co.uk

OPEN UNIVERSITY PRESS
McGraw - Hill Education

Coaching Skills
The definitive guide to being a coach
Fourth Edition

Jenny Rogers

ISBN: 978-0-335-26192-5(Paperback)
eBook: 978-0-335-26193-2
2016

This book has been a best seller for coaches all over the world since the first edition was published in 2004. Coaches appreciate its straightforward advice on how to coach and the truthful way the book captures the actual experience of coaching. This 4th edition has been extensively updated. It keeps the most popular features of earlier editions and also includes material on:

• The magic ingredients that determine whether the coach-client relationship works
• Why goal-setting and questioning are such important skills for any coach and how you can acquire them
• How to use the insights that are emerging from neuropsychology
• How as a coach you can work with clients to get them past their blocks and barriers
• How to cope with clients who cry or who report traumatic experience - and where the boundaries are with therapy
• How to give vital information - but in coaching style
• How to blend challenge with support
• Tips and hints on how to coach by phone
• A full template on how to run the first session

www.mheducation.co.uk

 OPEN UNIVERSITY PRESS
McGraw - Hill Education